The Harvard Guide to Careers in Mass Media

by John H. Noble

Office of Career Services
Harvard University
Cambridge, Massachusetts

The Harvard Guide to Careers in Mass Media

Acknowledgements

This book could not have been made possible without the cooperation of many Harvard alumni and other friends of Harvard who provided the author with advice and firsthand accounts of their experiences. My sincere thanks go to Steve Bell, Carlton Cuse, Jack Daley, Lee Daniels, Eric Ellenbogn, Mark Harris, Charles Hirschorn, Kurt Jacobsen, Mike Jensen, Robert Kraft, Jack Lemmon, Jim Lichtenberg, Gina Maccoby, Nancy K. Martin, Henry McGee, Robert Ellis Miller, Jack Noble, Tom Parry, Tom Pedulla, Rick Rosenthal, Jeff Sagansky, Polly Saltonstall, Nate Snyder, Mike Sobel, John Stimpson, and Robert Wise.

Special thanks go to Christina Covino, Larry Kahn, Elizabeth McNary, Stephanie Moffett, Frank Mungeam, Parker Reilly, Ron Roach, Cindy Rowe, and Adrienne Weiss, who provided the case studies.

Also, important contributors to the final product were Karen From, Susan Hadfield, and Martha Leape, who edited and proofread the text.

Trade Edition
Distributed exclusively by Bob Adams, Inc.

ISBN 1-55850-988-7

Preface

If you have taken the trouble to read even this much, then chances are the media intrigue you. Have you entertained the thought of starting a career in film, journalism, television, perhaps advertising? There is no doubt that careers in the media have definite appeal. The glamour, excitement, and challenge are hard to resist.

There is power in media. The meaning of "news" has been remarkably redefined by the different news organizations. What is newsworthy: crime, catastrophe, scandal, good deeds? Are our nation's officials elected by the people or do the news media predict and thereby select the winners for us?

The entertainment media have played an important role in shaping the moral sensibilities of its audience. Again, which force effects the change? Are the entertainers attempting to show us a reflection of ourselves, or are they introducing us to new and enticing adventures?

Promotional media, encompassing advertising, public relations, and corporate communications, are intended ideally to educate and inform the public. Have the ideals endured?

So, besides the glamour, excitement, and challenge of working in the media, there is the fact that, at many levels, you may have a great deal to do with the development of the public conscience, for its well-being or corruption. Successful people in all media share certain characteristics. They are totally committed to their fields and they have the discipline, confidence, and energy to persist. They realize that talent often goes unrewarded and is an elusive factor that cannot guarantee success. However, talent will always be an asset to someone chasing a career in the media.

This book aims to give the reader a practical introduction and realistic path to a career in the media. Each chapter explores a specific field with recommended steps for achieving the first goal: to gain entry into the field of your choice.

J.H.N.
Cambridge, MA

to Whitney

Contents

Introduction

How to Get a Job in the Mass Media

Read This First

You can always count on one thing when job hunting in the mass media: it will be a challenge. No matter what the state of the national economy at the time of your job search, the media industry will be highly competitive. For every job listing there will be a huge list of applicants. It makes getting into Harvard look easy.

However, don't let this fact discourage you. The strategy for getting into the media is not the same as the strategy for getting into Harvard. Once you learn the rules for breaking into your chosen media field, the task becomes more manageable, though still very challenging.

As you read the individual chapters which follow, always keep in mind the basic strategy described below. It should be applied to each of the fields within mass media. There are four basic steps that lead to jobs in media: the first step is research; the second involves making a comprehensive list of potential employers; contacting career advisers is the third step; and the fourth step is writing to the targeted employers, going for interviews and getting job offers or referrals to other employers.

Step One - Research and Preparation

Research

There are very few direct routes to a job in the media.

You will find few job listings, few training programs, few college recruiters on the college campuses. It becomes essential, therefore, to do some original source research. Talk with people in the industry and ask them how they got their jobs.

However, interviewing people in the industry should be done only after doing some basic research. You don't want to waste your and others' valuable time by interviewing for general information you can obtain on your own.

Start with career guides to get a sense for how the industry works. Your college's career office and most public libraries have a good selection of guides in their collections. Also, check the bibliography at the end of each of the following chapters.

At the same time, start a notebook by jotting down job titles and descriptions. Note key words, industry jargon, and any other items that seem especially important as your research progresses. This notebook will become a valuable tool when you proceed to the other steps in the job hunt.

Besides basic career guides, each industry has its own trade journal. By skimming through back issues of these magazines you will pick up valuable information about what is important inside the industry. You will read profiles not only of the "stars," but also about the behind-the-scenes people. Issues that have an impact on the future of the industry will be reported. You will read about new companies and new projects in the offing. Who won the industry awards last year? Which companies lost or went out of business?

Another interesting item to look at in the "trades" is the advertising. What companies and services advertise and why? You may uncover some segment of the industry not described in the career books you read. You may even find the name of a future employer. This is what you might call creative research.

Some of the trade magazines actually have job listings. Keep in mind, however, that if you see the job listing so will hundreds of others. In other words, don't count on securing a job or even an interview on a reply to a want-ad.

Once you have studied the trade magazines, you can use other sources such as *The Wall Street Journal* and *The New York Times*. The annual and other editions of the indexes for these two publications turn up interesting information about recent trends, mergers, acquisitions, start-ups. This news will be reported from the business perspective: especially helpful for those thinking about that side of an industry.

Large publicly held media organizations must publish annual financial reports for their stockholders. An "annual report" is a valuable source of information about a company. The part of the report written by the president or chairman can give an overall picture of how the company is doing and what its goals are in the years ahead. The report also lists key executives in the company; these names should be on your contact list. You can find annual reports in many large public libraries. Some cities have special business libraries.

Another source of information is so obvious that some job hunters don't think to pursue it. Because mass media is in the public eye, be sure to follow the media or medium in which your interests lie. If you want to get into the film industry, be sure to go to films. If you want to be a journalist, read a variety of newspapers. Future publishers should frequent the book stores. TV anchors should watch television news broadcasts. Etc., etc., etc. This research technique leads to the next part of the job-hunting discussion: preparation.

Preparation

Liberal arts students are born to worry about their careers. "Am I frittering away four years studying Shakespeare? I could be learning how to edit 16mm. film or to write advertising copy! What about technical schools? What am I doing pursuing such an impractical major?" Panic sets in. Wrinkles mount. Long distance calls to home . . . Stop!!

The fact is, for the kind of jobs most students are seeking, the academic training provided by the liberal arts is perfect preparation for a career in media. Any creative career requires an ability to analyze a wide variety of problems at the same time . . . to examine issues from many perspectives. Therefore, continue your study of Shakespeare in good health and take that same energy you spent worrying about your career and put it into pursuing your nonacademic interests.

Preparation for a career in mass media is best spent outside the classroom. In fact, because there is no real undergraduate training ground within a liberal arts program, it is essential to seek activities that allow some exposure to the media of your choice. It is important to explore the extracurricular activities on campus, the media organizations off campus, and to pursue any entrepreneurial ideas you may have early in your college career.

Extracurricular activities give you the opportunity to test your interests in the various media. Future journalists should try writing for one of the campus papers or magazines. Would-be radio announcers should try out for the campus radio station Those interested in television should do internships at the local TV stations. In other words, use your non academic time to explore the different media.

Because competition is so fierce for full-time work, you want to be pretty sure your goal is well-tested before you put all your energies into the job search. Also, this sort of preparation goes hand-in-hand with the research mentioned above. Future employers will expect that you have explored the media and they will look for some evidence that you understand what their businesses are like. They have no patience with people who "think" they might like to go into the media. They want a demonstrated commitment.

However, don't despair if you are reading this in the spring of your Senior year and have none of this work behind you. True, it would be easier if you had some experience, but there are ways to get it once you leave the ivied halls.

There are successful people in every phase of media who started in other professions or had no directly related experience in college. The job search becomes somewhat more challenging because you probably have to gain experience while holding down another job, but if the commitment is there you will find a way to reach your goal. One rule that is set in stone in the media is that there are no rules. Look in each of the following chapters for strategies to follow when experience is lacking upon graduation.

Graduate School

Graduate school is not a prerequisite for success in the media. However, there are good reasons to consider it. First, if you fall into the group of seniors who have very little experience in media, you may find that graduate school will help you get this experience.

Another reason for attending graduate school is to make contact with a large group of future colleagues and, perhaps, future employers that will become important in your career.

Graduate school, too, offers you the opportunity to really test your commitment to a career in the media. It will give you a good idea of what life will be like.

Step Two - Putting Together Your Target List

At this point in your search you should have assembled an impressive notebook. From your notes you should be able to put together a list of your top-choice employers. Perhaps this list will have 10 to 20 companies. Now, the challenge is to expand that list to include from 50 to 75 companies. Additional research using industry directories is the best way to expand your list.

Each sector of mass media (as defined by the chapter headings of this book) has its own industry directory; some even have more than one. These directories are often somewhat cryptic and difficult to use. However, with a little study, you can usually get at least the basic information necessary for writing an initial cover letter.

Many directories have alphabetical listings which include name, address, phone, the name of company executives, and a brief description of the company activities. Some directories have geographic, subject, and/or functional indexes. Most public libraries have these directories in their collections.

Your list should be arranged alphabetically for easy reference. Include the necessary information for a cover letter: contact name, company name and address, and a brief description of the company. Use one page of your growing job-hunting notebook for each company on your list. Also keep a list of your top 10 choices.

With a jam-packed notebook, filled with information and a list of potential employers, you are now ready to contact your career advisers.

Step Three - Contacting Career Advisers

At this point you might wonder why you shouldn't simply write letters to the 50 employers on your list. Mailing now might produce good results, but it is more likely that you will be disappointed by the return on your time, energy, and investment in the Postal Service.

Most media professionals rely heavily on their personal contacts and relationships to accomplish their best work. Often, picking up the phone is the most effective way to get results: calling a friend for advice or a favor, getting the latest information on new projects, testing out a new idea, and searching for new employees. Therefore, if your adviser looks at your list and can refer you to people he or she knows, you will greatly improve the return on your job hunting efforts.

The task, then, is to assemble a list of advisers. The first place to begin is to enlist the advice of any family or other personal contacts. Many of you may cringe at the thought of using family connections to get a start in your career. After all, if you're not good enough to make it on your own, then how good are you? However, because getting a job in media is so difficult, you will never get a job simply because of someone you know. In the end, you will have to make a good impression and win the job because of your own merits. So, view any contacts you may have as valuable sources of information and as people who can refer you to those in hiring positions.

Next, look to people you know in the university setting. Many professors are quite familiar with the media because of their research activities. Harvard professors frequently appear on television, talk on radio, publish magazine articles and books, consult on filmmaking projects, and are generally involved in one medium or another. There may be faculty advisers to student media groups that could become resources. In other words, don't overlook the faculty because there is no academic department that deals with media.

College alumni are a very valuable source of career information and guidance. Your college's career office or alumni office should have information about how to contact alumni. Alumni will not necessarily know about job openings. However, if you appear to be a committed and talented prospect, an alumnus will probably try to help you in whatever way possible.

Now, with the list of alumni advisers adding even more pages to your notebook, start work on a strategy for contacting them. The best approach is usually a well-constructed cover letter with an accompanying resume. This approach will give the adviser notice that you will be calling and time to think about your questions.

The letter should be friendly and full of information about why you're interested in talking to them and what kind of media experience you've had in school. Tell them when you will be calling and that you look forward to getting their advice. Don't worry if the letter spills over to a second page, but try to limit it there. Your adviser will be happy to help you, especially if you have done your homework and seem truly interested in his or her career field.

The goal in contacting several advisers is to set up a series of appointments in which you can get the advice firsthand. Meeting in person makes a big difference, both for you and the adviser. As mentioned above, media is a "people" business. The personal contact will make you more than just a voice over the phone. Also, it emphasizes your commitment to the search.

When you visit with the adviser, be sure to bring with you the notebook you have been developing and samples of any appropriate work you have done: newspaper articles, short film clips, advertising copy, press releases, posters -- any tangible evidence of work done in the media. If you don't have any materials, be ready for the advice that suggests you get to work on some. Don't forget to show the adviser your contact list. He or she may be able to edit and add to your list and, as mentioned above, perhaps act as a referral.

You should have two goals when meeting with an adviser: the first is to establish a good working relationship, and the second is to get a lead to the next step in your job hunt. Getting a lead can consist of a name of some other adviser or employer to contact, advice about materials you should create, or, if you're lucky, information about a specific job opening. Try never leave yourself at a dead end.

Step Four - Contacting Employers

With your notebook full of information edited by your advisers, you should now be ready to take the final step and approach your potential employers. Your approach should be similar to your contacts with advisers; however, there are a few important differences.

The Cover Letter

The cover letter is one of the most important elements of successful job hunting. It gives you the opportunity to set yourself apart from the vast majority of job seekers who start their letters: "This June I will be graduating from Harvard and plan to enter a career in television."

Your cover letter should be dynamic, creative, and fun or at least interesting to read. Don't ask for a job! Ask for advice and information. Tell them about your commitment to media and what you have done so far to demonstrate that commitment. State your long-term goal and make it clear that you're willing to start at the bottom to get there. Mention why you are writing to them in particular. Say that you'd like only 20-30 minutes of their time. Tell them that you will be calling their office in a week to set up an appointment. The letter should make the person reading want to meet you. They should be thinking, "This sounds like an interesting newcomer I should meet." The best book on this subject is *Executive Jobs Unlimited* by Carl Boll which has an excellent chapter on writing cover letters.

The Meeting

Be prepared! You have gone to all the trouble of setting up a series of meetings; now, make the most of them. Your goal in this type of meeting is to get one of three things: a job, another meeting, or a referral.

Be clear about your career goal and think about the possible routes to that goal. The person sitting across from you should get a sense of commitment and seriousness of purpose. Convince them that you are going to do whatever it takes to get started.

Also, be sure to ask your contact about his or her career. There is no better way to get sympathy for your cause than by reminding the person how he or she began in the business.

At the end of the meeting ask if there are other people with whom you should talk. If your contact seems interested, end your conversation by saying that you'll stay in touch about the progress of your job search. Make a good impression, be positive, be someone with whom the employer would like to work. A short thank-you note should follow your meeting.

Network Strategy

The main strategy behind the four steps just described is to create a never-ending network of contacts. After each meeting, you should have a lead that turns into another meeting. Eventually, you will find a job. Planning, of course, is essential in this process. Arrange long distance trips to include several meetings; leave time in your schedule to make unexpected appointments; plan a budget that will give you enough time to fully explore the opportunities. Exactly when you find a job will depend upon how quickly you pursue contacts and how many people you see.

What Follows

In the following chapters you will read about specific areas of mass media. Each chapter will begin with a basic industry profile and the career profiles for liberal arts grads. The discussion will go on to include job-hunting tips specific to that industry, including a case study of a recent Harvard graduate's job hunt in the field, and a bibliography of major reference works. Keep this introduction in mind when reading.

Chapter 1

Film & Television

It's a high risk profession ... you must assume that with whatever your intelligence and your ability or training, that you must also have a very dumb spot in your mind. You must be able to face the fact that if someone says, "Okay, I ran everything through a computer; your chances of making a living as a career, let alone what your fantasies may be; your chances are a million to one." You must be dumb enough to say, "That's fine. Yeah, I'll do it, I'll make it." Without that stupidity, that blind stupidity, you will never make it.
- Jack Lemmon, Actor, Producer, Director

It is ironic that the motion picture and television industry[1] is so mysterious. One would think that an industry so much in the public eye could be well defined by even the most casual spectator. The fact remains, however, that few people outside the industry understand how a major television show or motion picture is produced.

Industry Profile

The dynamics of the film and television industry have changed a great deal in the past fifteen years. The major studios and television networks no longer take on a slate of pictures or sign contracts with directors for seven or eight years. Each film or TV series is a completely separate project. The Majors (major motion

---

[1]Career paths in film and non-news television are very similar and will be discussed together here. Those interested in television news should read Chapter Four.

picture companies) and Networks primarily provide the financing and distribution in partnership with an independent producer, very much the way a bank agrees to provide capital for a real estate project: however, with more creative input.

A good way to determine a particular company's structure is to look at the breakdown of administrative positions as outlined in *The Hollywood Creative Directory*, *The International Motion Picture Almanac*, and *The International Television Almanac*. The following depicts a typical corporate ladder, but keep in mind that each corporation has its own variations:

I. Film Division

    A. Chairman of the Board
       President
       Chairman, Executive Committee
       Vice Chairman of the Board
       Vice President and General Manager
       Vice President, Business Affairs

    B. Production
       Vice President, Worldwide Production
       Vice President, Studio Operations
       Executive Production Manager
       Vice President, Production Business Affairs
       Vice President, Studio Operations
       Senior Story Executive
    Heads of: Property, Music, Sound, Engineering, Purchasing, Wardrobe, Film Editing, Make-up, Transportation, Construction

II. Television Division

    A. President
       Vice President, Business Affairs

B. Vice President, Programs
   Vice President, Program Development
   Vice President, Live/Tape and Special Projects

C. Sales
   Vice President, Syndication Sales
   Vice President, Domestic Sales
   Vice President, International Media
   Regional Sales Managers

D. Publicity, Advertising and Promotions

Large independent production companies are not normally affiliated with the Majors, although they can rent production facilities (soundstages, studios, equipment, etc.) from them. Independent production companies may be quite large with full production staffs, or very small, frequently calling upon freelance experts in all divisions. They may be either producers of major feature films, such as LucasFilm, Tri-Star, and Thorn EMI or producers of prime-time television programming, such as Norman Lear, MTM Enterprises, Quinn Martin, and Lorimar Productions. Independent producers may be specialists in producing commercials, documentaries, educational or industrial films.

The large production companies which produce major motion pictures or prime-time programming are primarily located in the Los Angeles area and, secondarily, in New York City. However, filmmaking is going on to some degree in all parts of the country. Again, *The Hollywood Creative Directory* and *Motion Picture Almanac* is a good source for locating the Independents. **Back Stage's** *Annual Film and Tape Directory* provides even more detailed information about the "Indies."

In addition to the Majors and Independents, the

talent agency holds an important role in motion picture development. The agent is the primary representative of the industry's creative force. The actor in front of the screen, the director, and the writer who provides the material on which the entire industry depends, are most often represented by agents. The leading talent agencies include the William Morris Agency, International Creative Management, and Creative Artists Agency, which have offices in Los Angeles and New York.

Salary

High risk = high reward. This is the typical equation for the film/TV job market. At entry level, no one considers that you are taking a very big risk, so your reward is relatively small. Typical starting salaries for those hunting for a production assistant job might be anything from zero to something in the mid teens.

Those who can land a job at a major studio might expect something a little closer to $20,000 and, if really lucky, as much as $25,000. Be prepared to "pay your dues" for a while. Fortunately, once you prove yourself, the higher salaries will follow. Just remember: save your money for that rainy day when you may be standing in the unemployment line.

Career Profiles and Job-Hunting Tips

There are three keys to gaining entry into this highly competitive field. The first is to study and learn the language of the industry. The second is to decide which aspect of filmmaking meets your career goals. The third, and perhaps most important key, is acting on the knowledge gained, and persevering until success is achieved.

The First Key: The Language

It is absolutely essential that you learn as much

about the film and television industry as you can before writing your first job letter. Obviously, it is impossible to know as much as those already in the business, but you can come close.

There are some very clear steps to becoming conversant in "film language." Begin your self-taught course in film by reading *Getting Into Film* by Mel London and *The Cool Fire* by Bob Shanks. These two books, written by experienced professionals, will give you an idea of the basic structure and ambiance of the industry. Then subscribe to *Weekly Variety* and read the film and television sections thoroughly. You may even want to go one step further and read *The Hollywood Reporter*.

If you haven't been viewing many films or popular TV shows, make it a habit to watch one new film and one new TV show a week. Start a personal notebook of your favorite films, TV shows, directors, producers, actors, and studios. Read *American Film Magazine* and *Premiere*. Study The *Hollywood Creative Directory*, the *Motion Picture and Television Almanacs* and learn who's who in the industry.

Try to get your hands on some TV scripts and screenplays, through your local library or film school. Read *Back Stage* magazine. Make a list of all the new films that are scheduled to start production; there are weekly lists in *Variety*. In other words, become a fanatic. Perhaps you already qualify as one. That's a good sign.

Before long you will learn the basic structure of the industry. You will learn the differences and relationship between the Hollywood Majors (Paramount, Twentieth Century Fox, Universal, Columbia Pictures, MGM, United Artists, and Warner Brothers) and the many independent producers.

Becoming a film fanatic, though, is only the first step

in gaining insight. With a good avocational knowledge of film you can pass what might be called "Film Language I." At this point you should be getting a feeling for what part of the industry intrigues you most. Are you a director, a producer, an actor, a writer? Or, would you like to be all of these things? It's possible. However, you have to start somewhere.

The Second Key: Setting Your Goal

The Producer

The key to producing is to find good material. The major decision is what project to start with. You must have a keen sense for material.
- *Robert Wise, Producer and Director*
  (work includes: West Side Story, Sound of Music)

A producer deals with ideas. He or she is responsible for getting the multi-million dollar project under way. The producer is the one on the lookout for talent. Finding an exciting script, talented directors and cinematographers, and a willing financial backer is an essential part of a producer's job. A producer must have an exceptional knack for "story." What is conflict? What touches people? What is entertaining? As Tom Parry, a Hollywood producer, states: "You are in the business of creating taste." If you like this process of discovery and speculation, then you may enjoy the life of a producer. You must have the entrepreneurial spirit.

It is difficult to give a general description of the kind of person who does well at producing. The qualities mentioned above are essential, but how do you develop good taste? Perhaps the best way to develop a sense of taste is to experiment. Find out what people think of your ideas and concepts. The best way to get an audience for this "taste-testing" process is to create products for them to judge, any products.

24

Find a play that you think is good and produce it. Invent a product . . . a poster, a T-shirt, a bumper sticker. Then figure out a way to get it made, advertise or publicize it and see what happens. Did you lose your shirt, break even, or make a million? It doesn't really matter what the outcome is if you learn something about how people think.

Put together a musical group, work with it, promote it, organize a concert. What's that? You don't play an instrument? So what . . . it's the idea that counts and your ability to present that idea to the public. Remember, a producer finds talent, finds good ideas. You don't necessarily have to be the "talent" to be a good producer.

Mike Medavoy offered me a job to be his assistant. He was a top executive for United Artists. Being naive I said that I really wanted to be on location learning how to make movies, not in the office pushing papers. Medavoy said very candidly that the business is not how to make movies . . . it's how to make deals, how to put projects together. I learned a great deal in my three years at United Artists.
- Tom Parry, Producer

The Director

"If you want to be a filmmaker, make a film." This piece of straightforward advice comes from Rick Rosenthal, a major motion picture director who did not direct his first major film, *Halloween II*, until the age of 29. To quote him further: "That was about the right age for me to finally have the chance to direct." For a young would-be director these words of wisdom are discouraging. What happens until you get the chance to direct your first major film?

Learn the craft of filmmaking. If you can make a film while you are still in school, that film can be the start of your training. The film itself does not have to be a full-length masterpiece. It can be in 8 mm. and as short as eight minutes. However, the film must demonstrate your talent, your style, and your taste in filmmaking.

Don't think that you have to come up with a completely original piece of work for your first film. Pick a subject that you know well and feel confident directing.

Do a good piece of work. Do a scene from Sophie's Choice and do it well. Perhaps not Shakespeare, but a scene from Arthur Miller, Tennessee Williams. There's literate work to be done that has been respected in the theater and in films. Show us the ability to stage a scene, or write a scene, or photograph a scene.

    - Robert Ellis Miller, Director
    (Reuben Reuben, Heart is a Lonely Hunter)

Robert Wise, director of two Academy Award winners, suggests that aspiring directors get some acting experience while they are in school, simply to learn as much as possible about the final product.

Remember that you do not have to attend a film school to prepare for a career as a director. In fact, many established directors encourage getting as broad a background as possible in all academic disciplines while in school in order to gain valuable perspective necessary to insightful filmmaking.

There is a trap in specializing; you can cut out other areas that are of tremendous benefit. If you were a bright young person at the age of 16 or 17 with talent, who really knew what you wanted, you might say, "Why go to college? I might as well go out and get some professional experience." Very bad; don't ever do it. You are limiting yourself. You are limiting your mind, your ability to understand other points of view; you lose exposure. It's like saying you don't have to travel. But go ahead . . . try to play an Italian who lives in Italy. Boy, you are

behind the eight ball. It is tremendously valuable to be exposed to things that have nothing to do, apparently, with the craft you are interested in.
- *Jack Lemmon*

The director interprets the script and develops it from its initial stages through to the final editing processes. A director may work on one film for a year or more. If directing if your goal, then be prepared to go through an extensive apprenticeship. Many leading directors in film world of today did not direct their first film until past the age of thirty.

The Writer

The single, simplest way into the business is to be a talented writer.
- *Robert Wise*

Everything starts with the script. The screenwriter must have the inspiration, dedication, discipline, and talent to create a story that will engage and appeal to a wide audience. One producer remarked that there are probably only five or six really talented comedy writers in Los Angeles at any one time. These are not very good odds for betting on a career as a writer.

However, if you are a writer or think you would like to be one, don't give up. Write a play and try to get it produced. A good test of your ability to persevere as a writer is your willingness to go out and try to "sell" your project. Find a campus producer who needs a play. Try a local theater group. If you can't get anyone to produce your play, at least get someone to read it: film professors, English professors, roommates. Approach anyone whose opinion you respect. Then be ready for criticism. Don't be discouraged by initial bad reviews. Learn what elements are missing in your story and hang on to those that receive praise. It will probably take five or six attempts to create something with which you are really happy.

If your goal is to write screenplays that become major motion pictures, then you must keep in mind what commercial value your work has. No studio will touch a project that will not guarantee a solid group of viewers. Study the filmmaking market and read the trade journals (*Screenwriter's Digest, Variety, Back Stage*). Read as many produced scripts as you can by visiting your local public library or film school library. If no scripts are available, then take a screenwriting course. Learn the techniques of scriptwriting so that when you are ready to submit your masterpiece, it will look professional.

Keep in mind that successful screenwriters come from varied backgrounds. You need not be an honors English major to be a good screenwriter. Developing your appreciation for the elements of a good story and dedicating yourself to your writing will get you started in the right direction. There are no guaranteed prescriptions to success as a writer. However, if you can persist in spite of this uncertainty and the terrible odds, that will carry you a long way towards your goal.

The above-mentioned career goals describe only a small fraction of the many different kinds of careers available within the motion picture/television industry. However, getting your first job will depend largely on how you define your ultimate goal. Knowing where your interests lie in relation to the three major positions mentioned above will help you pick your starting point. Most likely, you will have to make contact with the people who are in the positions mentioned above. Unfortunately, there isn't enough room to mention all the various types of positions. Again, *Getting Into Film* by Mel London and *Opportunities in Television and Video* by Maxine and Robert Reed are two books that provide the kind of detail you should seek after reading this chapter.

The Third Key: Using What You Know to Get Your First Job

I always knew what I wanted to do. I did plays in the dramatic clubs. I acted as a teenager in off-Broadway. It's a most difficult business to break into and it's really based, to a terrible degree, on contacts . . . Total dedication is necessary. There can be no alternatives . . . nothing you can do except to pursue a career in film.
- Robert Ellis Miller, Director

Job hunting in the film industry can be discouraging and frustrating because there is no direct path you can follow that leads to success. Each person you talk to seems to have arrived at the destination using a different form of transportation. So the question becomes, "Where do I begin?"

I've Got a Little List

Actually, if you talk to enough people in the film/ television industry, you find that while there are no two routes alike, they share common characteristics. The first, most important aspect is getting the product, you, in front of the potential employer. Successful job hunters in the industry talk to a lot of people. They talk to agents, producers, directors, studio executives: anyone who may have or know about a job.

You should attend any lectures, seminars, or work-shops in which filmmakers or television professionals participate. Stay after the lecture and introduce yourself.

If you can show the person that you know a great deal about film or TV, you might just be impressive enough to win a meeting.

Join a local film society. Learn all about what is being done in film around your area. Chances are you will meet a fair number of would-be filmmakers like you, looking for a job. However, many societies sponsor special events. If you can become a part of the organizing group, you can then become responsible for bringing professional filmmakers to visit your group. Contacting people in the industry becomes somewhat easier as a representative of a group than as an individual.

After exploring all of the avenues just mentioned, you may have quite a list of people. They might not be the right people, however. Go one step further in your hunt for contacts. Study the corporate structure of the Majors by looking at *The Hollywood Creative Directory*, *The Motion Picture* and *Television Almanacs*. Look for the names of the Director of Production, the Director of Publicity, or a Director of any department. Those just below the chief executives are the people who have the power to hire. Don't try for the chief executives unless you like investing in postage stamps. They are very, very difficult to reach and very rarely available for appointments.

Be sure to read *Variety* and the *Hollywood Reporter* to get the latest news about changes in the ranks of the prominent filmmakers and television executives. *The Hollywood Creative Directory*, *The Motion Picture and Television Almanacs* are good resources, but they are often out-of-date as soon as they are published. It is not unusual for a studio to turn over its executive staff several times a year!

Keep *Variety* handy because each week there is a list of films going into production, including the production companies' names, addresses and sometimes the name of the producers. Every time a new film or TV series goes into production, jobs are being created. This weekly list will also keep you up-to-date on the current trends. Keep track of what kinds of films are being produced. If you look in a publication called *The Ross Reports*, published by Television Index Inc. in New York, you will be able to keep up on the latest news about primetime TV shows. You may soon find out what material is popular with the studio and TV execs.

Armed with the list, you are now ready to take Hollywood by storm!

The Hollywood Letter

The letter you write to these 150 people will have to be the best letter you can write. Forget about a resume. Resumes tend to be much too impersonal for those in Hollywood. A film or TV executive is looking for someone who is pleasant to work with, someone who can be counted on, and someone creative who has something to offer. A resume cannot reflect all of these traits: A good letter can.

Write a letter that makes statements (true, of course) about your accomplishments. Don't boast; state facts and results. Let the reader draw his or her own conclusions. Keep your paragraphs short and limited to one idea; make the tone enthusiastic. Show that you have potential. Make the reader want to meet you. Close the letter by saying that you would like to arrange a meeting and that you will call within the week. Also, don't forget to mention in your first paragraph the name of the person who referred you. If you need more help in writing the letter, refer to an excellent book entitled *Executive Jobs Unlimited* and read the chapter on broadcast letters.

If you wrote a good letter and made a good impression, you should receive ten to fifteen replies. Don't get excited; no one will have a job for you solely as a result of your letter. However, out of the fifteen or so replies you receive, perhaps ten will agree to a meeting.[2] Congratulations, you have passed "Film Language II"!

Hollywood, Here I Come!

With the offer of ten possible meetings, you should now plan your trip to Los Angeles. If at all possible, plan to stay for at least six months. The job hunt might last that long or longer. Call your ten prospects and set up specific meeting times. Be persistent in arranging your appointments. Be pleasant to the assistant or secretary answering the phone and ask for his or her name. If that person likes you, you will have a better chance of reaching the person in charge. Try calling during lunch or late in the afternoon when the secretary is likely to be out. Perhaps the boss will answer. People in film and TV count on you to be persistent because they often do not have the time to return phone calls or write letters. Persistence is rewarded in Hollywood.

Buy your one-way ticket to Los Angeles. Yes . . . do it! It's what you might call "Making the Commitment." A trip to Los Angeles is paramount, if you'll excuse the pun.

You must absolutely go to Los Angeles!
- Robert Wise, Director

You are fooling around if you don't go to L.A.
-Carlton Cuse, Universal Studios

---

[2]If you receive no replies, you will have to follow up your letters with some phone calls. Be persistent and you should be rewarded with some appointments.

The industry is impossible to understand or enter from anywhere except Los Angeles.
-Charles Hirschorn, The Mount Company

Coming to Los Angeles is one of the first tests of your commitment to a career in the industry.
-Tom Parry, Producer

Once you have established yourself in Los Angeles and had your phone connected with a phone answering machine or answering service, you are ready to begin the final phase of your job hunt.[3]

The Meeting

Now that you have a few interviews set up and are settled in Los Angeles, you may think that you can relax a bit and enjoy the beaches. Not so. When you go into a meeting with a senior management type at a major studio, network station, or independent production house, you had better have something to show. Remember, you have to sell yourself and your abilities. If you want to write, bring a script. If you want to produce, bring an unproduced script or film that you like or have discovered. If you want to direct, bring your own film.

If your aim is to be a writer, one prominent Hollywood screenwriter suggests that you write something that shows your abilities. Don't write something imita-

---

[3]A phone machine might seem extravagant for someone in the throes of a difficult job hunt, however, it is absolutely essential that people have some way to reach you. Put another way -- they will probably only call once.

tive. Be original, but be commercial. Your script will probably not be produced, but it may lead to assignments from directors or producers on speculation. Take every opportunity to submit material. Write to Writer's Guild East or Writer's Guild West for lists of agents who will read unsolicited scripts.

If your aim is to produce, then produce some talent for your interviewer. While Charles Hirschorn, current Director of Script Development at the Mount Company, was job hunting, he spent time at the local film schools looking for talented young filmmakers and writers. He found a few scripts and presented them to his interviewers as examples of his taste. Be resourceful and creative. If you can dig up talent, you will be a valuable person in any organization.

If your goal is to direct, have your film ready on video tape.[4] As with writers, don't imitate. Do a project that reflects your best work. Be ready to discuss your ideas of good filmmaking. Do your homework by viewing your interviewer's latest project.

Know What You Want

If you are successful in your interview, you will be asked to discuss your goals. Be specific. Mention your long-term goals, but have an immediate goal that is a real job. Don't say that you would accept anything available (even though you should be ready to do so). Mention a job title, such as "reader," "production assistant," "story editor," "executive assistant," or "development assistant." By doing this, you are letting your interviewer know that

---

[4]Most producers or directors have video tape players available for viewing work in progress. Also, video tape is much easier to handle than film.

you have realistic goals; he or she will be better able to point you in the right direction.

After a good interview you should either have a job offer, another interview appointment, or a referral. You want to avoid dead ends. If a job doesn't come within the first few weeks, find any part-time job that will bring you some financial security and a break from the rigorous job-hunting process. Keep at it and you will succeed. When you succeed, celebrate and then get to work. You will have just started one of the most exciting and challenging careers possible.

Film School

For those of you who cannot quite bring yourself to just pull up all roots and head West, there are alternatives. However, before you consider these alternatives, you should really do some soul-searching about your desire to enter the film/TV industry. There is probably no other industry as insecure as the motion picture/television industry. Getting fired is a common occurrence. In fact, if you haven't been fired at least once in your career, it would be unusual. Therefore, if you are looking for a more secure route into the industry, you may be looking at the wrong career.

However, there is one route that will let you explore the film industry and thus let you make a wise career choice without suffering constant insecurity.

There are five or six top film schools in the nation that will give you a good idea of life in Hollywood. They are: The University of Southern California, New York University, California Institute of the Arts, The American Film Institute, and the University of California at Los Angeles. All schools are competitive to enter. Some require that you have done some previous film work and that you submit a film with your application. If you can get into film school, there is no guarantee that you will get a job upon graduation. However, you will be working in an active community of filmmakers, and contact between the industry and the film schools is good. You will be in one of the best environments from which to launch your career. Refer to *The Guide to College Courses in Film and TV* published by the Peterson's Guides for detailed information about programs around the country.

Film as Art

One producer emphasized that in Hollywood the term is "Show Business" and not "Show Art." There is a concentration on the commerciality of any project. Because millions of dollars are invested in each major motion picture, there is a real concern for making a return.

There are alternatives to big projects though. It should be pointed out again that filmmaking is going on in all parts of the country. Documentaries, educational films, government films, and industrial training films are examples of the filmmaking in which Hollywood producers have little interest.

Therefore, if you are a true filmmaker at heart and want your film to be your film and you shy away from the bright lights of Hollywood, there is important work for you to do. You should use many of the same job-hunting techniques described above, except focus on particular film genres. You may even be that rare, resourceful artist who is the true "independent" filmmaker and become your own film company. Create films by raising support and funds through grants and other sources. Read *The Independent*, a trade magazine designed for the small independent filmmaker. *How to Enter and Win Film Contests* by Alan Gadney may be of some use.

Alternatives

If you have trouble entering the industry and want at least some vicarious contact, there are more routes to explore. Develop your writing skills and become associated with the press as a reviewer. (See Chapter 3.) Or, get into advertising where the creation of TV commercials demands constant concern for film production. Filmmakers who work on doing commercials often find their way to Hollywood. Explore government agencies. They produce hundreds of films a year on a myriad of subjects. Large educational institutions often have media departments with film and video tape production services. Comb through the various film directories mentioned in the bibliography and you may discover multiple ways of creating a career which involves filmmaking.

Case Study

Christina Covino, Scriptwriter

As an undergraduate, Chris spent a good deal of her time as manager of Harvard's Track & Cross Country Teams and as an English concentrator. She also found time to write. She had something to show when she made her trip West. She is now assistant to the producer of St. Elsewhere and continues working on her scriptwriting skills.

During my senior year, I decided that I would pursue a career in the entertainment industry. My particular interest is screenwriting, but I wanted to move to Los Angeles and get any job in television/film in order to learn more about it.

To begin, I did some preliminary research at the Office of Career Services. After meeting with the counselor specializing in media, I followed up his advice and checked the alumni files. I wrote down all of the names, addresses, and phone numbers of Harvard graduates, living in Southern California and working in television or film.

During spring break, I went to Los Angeles to meet some of these people and get advice. A month or so in advance, I had written to them, and made follow-up calls. Almost everybody was helpful and friendly, and agreed to meet me to offer advice. I had fifteen appointments set up before I even got to California. I had also contacted people who were friends of friends, and involved in the entertainment industry; any contact helps. Still, I didn't have many of my own "personal" contacts, so the alumni files were a lifesaver.

The spring break left me very enthusiastic because everyone seemed particularly nice and helpful. I learned that it was impossible to secure a job three months in advance, when I hadn't moved to California yet. Nevertheless, each meeting was successful if, out of it, I gained a few more names of people to contact.

Three days after graduation, I hopped in the car and headed West. Upon my arrival in Los Angeles, I found things were somewhat different. It is easy to get advice, but not as easy to get a job. Still, it is important to go around and meet as many people as possible, because one of those people just might remember you when a job opening does occur.

On interviews I stressed that I was willing to start at the bottom. (People tend to fear that a Harvard graduate wants to take over the company within two weeks!) I tried to be personable and friendly, so that potential employers would want to work with me.

It took me six weeks to get a job, and I'm told I was lucky. I didn't feel lucky when I was trudging around Hollywood and the Valley, running out of money, living on generic macaroni and cheese, trying to find a cock-roach-free apartment. I worked temp jobs, to earn money and meet prospective employers. One Harvard alum gave me freelance work analyzing books and scripts which also helped me learn about development.

Finally, I got a call from another alumnus whom I'd met a few weeks previously. He told me about another Harvard graduate who was about to start two TV movies and needed an assistant. He also called ahead, giving him my name, so that my call was expected. I met him that afternoon, and the next day I was hired.

I worked as "Assistant to the Producer" on those two TV movies, *Crime of Innocence* and *Under Siege*. It was a terrific first job. After the shows finished production, the producers decided to keep me on in their development department, so I was able to learn about another aspect of the television/film industry.

After a year of working for that company, I felt I had learned as much as I could from them, and needed a change. With a year's experience, it was much easier to apply for a job within the industry. Through an ad in *Variety* I got my current job, as Assistant to the Producers of St. Elsewhere, at MTM Enterprises. It's basically secretarial work, but I have a lot of potential to move up, and I also have plenty of free time to write.

As for my writing, I'm trying to build up a portfolio now, with spec scripts. ["Spec scripts" are written as examples of your best work. Only rarely do they get produced.] Breaking into writing is almost as difficult as breaking into acting. No one will even read a writer's work unless she has an agent, and it takes a while for an agent to evaluate the work, if he agrees to read it in the first place.

I still haven't "made it" in Hollywood, and I won't feel I have until I've sold my first script. When that happens, however, the payoff, in personal satisfaction as well as financial satisfaction, will be worth it.

Bibliography

Books

Adventures in the Screen Trade, William Goldman, Warner Books, New York, 1982.
One man's view of the world of feature filmmaking/dealmaking. An entertaining and informative view of the film industry.

Career Opportunities in Television and Video, Maxine and Robert Reed, Facts On File Publications, New York, 1982.
A useful listing of job titles with career paths for each job title. Gives job description, salary, educational or experience necessary, and a career ladder telling what the next career step may be.

Cool Fire, Bob Shanks, Vintage Books, New York, 1976.
One man's view of the world of prime-time television. A good book from which to glean some of the cultural aspects of working in the entertainment business.

Creative Careers, Gary Blake and Robert Bly, Wiley Press, New York, 1983.
Excellent chapters on Television and Film. Very good bibliographies.

Dream Jobs, Gary Blake and Robert Bly, Wiley Press, New York, 1985.
An insightful description of various career fields, including a chapter on cable television. Has a very good bibliography for each chapter.

Executive Jobs Unlimited, Carl R. Boll, MacMillan Publishing Co., New York, New York, 1979.
Provides a strategy to job hunting particularly appropriate to the film and television industries. Especially important is the chapter on cover letters.

Getting into Film, Mel London, Ballantine Books, New York, 1977.
An excellent introduction to the film industry and all its different facets, including a section on job hunting. Read this book first.

Inside Track, Ross and Kathryn Petras, Vintage Books, New York, 1986.
Focuses on individual companies, some in the entertainment business, including Warner Brothers, the Networks.

Directories

1989 Internships, F&W Publications, Cincinnati, Ohio, annual.
Describes internships and summer jobs in film and television, along with other categories. Eligibility and application information for each listing.

The American Film Institute Guide to College Courses in Film and Television, Peterson's Guides, Princeton, New Jersey, 1980.

Back Stage Film & Tape Directory, Back Stage Publications, New York, annual.

Lists film and videotape producers around the coun try. Lists primarily those companies or individuals involved in the actual production work.

Broadcasting's Yearbook, Broadcasting Publications Washington, D.C., annual.

Valuable information about the television and radio industries, including market statistics, station addresses, phone numbers, and other pertinent details about broadcasting. Compliments the TV Factbooks.

Directors Guild Directory, Directors Guild of Amei ca, New York, New York, annual.

Lists addresses and phone numbers of all members of the Directors Guild of America. Also lists agents and award winners.

Getting Work Experience, Betsy Bauer, Dell Publishing, New York, New York, 1985.

Among other listings, describes summer internship programs in television and film. Gives pertinent application information including pay scale (if any), qualifications desired, and deadlines

The Hollywood Creative Directory, 451 Kelton Ave., Los Angeles, CA 90024, three times a year.

An insider's guide to the entertainment business in Los Angeles, with names and addresses of companies and the key executives in each. Probably the most up-to-date and comprehensive guide available.

International Motion Picture Almanac, Quigley Publishing Company, New York, annual.

Contains who's who of prominent individuals in the motion picture industry (many of whom also appear in the Television Almanac), lists of studios, independent producers and related services and suppliers.

International Television Almanac, Quigley Publishing Company, New York, annual.

Contains who's who of prominent individuals in the television community, lists of television companies, and producers, as well as other information and listings about industry-related suppliers.

The Student Guide to Mass Media Internships, Vol. 2, Ronald Claxton, Intern Research Group, University of Colorado, Boulder, Colorado, annual.

List internships available in television (and other areas) with requirements, pay scales and deadlines.

Periodicals

American Film, American Film Institute, New York, New York, monthly.

The magazine for film buffs. A good summary of recent news in the film industry.

Back Stage, BackStage Publications, New York, New York, weekly.

Trade magazine devoted primarily to communications and entertainment news. Good sections on film and television. Supplements *Variety.*

The Ross Reports, Television Index Inc., New York, New York, monthly.

Primarily a resource for actors; lists all prime-time, day-time, and news programs with information about production locations, producers' names, and format. Also has four-page "blue" section with late-breaking news about new shows and TV movies.

Variety, Variety Inc., New York, New York, daily in New York and Los Angeles, otherwise weekly. The industry trade magazine. Read this!

Chapter 2

The Music Business

If you think the business is exciting, glamorous, reward-
ing, you're right. It is. It also has its full share of finks and
phonies, and its own adequate quota of trials and travail for
anyone who wants to make progress in it.
- Joseph Csida, The Music/Record Career Handbook

Industry and Career Profiles

Record Companies

The music industry (here primarily concerned with popular music) has gone through periods of ups and downs in the past twenty years. It experienced phenomenal growth since the 60's due mostly to the popularity of rock music. From 1976 to 1978, the industry grew by 70 percent, topping $4 billion in sales. However, starting in 1979, it went through several years of "depression" due to lack of consumer demand. Hundreds of people lost their jobs and many of the smaller companies went out of business.

Only since 1983 has the industry started to recover. The banner year was 1985 when sales again peaked $4 billion to reach a new high. Although the outlook is good for the music business, people in the industry are still very cautious because of the recent downturn.

Two companies, CBS/Records and Warner Brothers Records, represent nearly half of domestic industry sales. Other companies filling in a major part of the industry include Capitol, MCA, PolyGram, RCA and A&M. There are many smaller companies that specialize in certain genres. The music industry encompasses a great deal, too much for our discussion here. The focus of this chapter will be on the recording and radio industries and on careers found most popular by those with a background in liberal arts. Those interested in becoming recording artists, songwriters, and performers should consult the bibliography for other more in-depth studies.

Perhaps the best way to describe the types of careers possible in a record company is to explore the origins of the albums in your own record collection.

The life of a new record begins in the Artists & Repertoire (A&R) department of a record company. (Also see the section below on the Music Publisher.) This is one place where new talent is found and the project begins. Executives in this department spend most of their time listening to music: night club performances, concerts, other companies' records, and hundreds of demo tapes a week. This may sound like an ideal job; however, it involves a great deal of risk.

You must have a deep knowledge of everything that is happening now. You then try to extrapolate from that. There is this great big context out there. You must be able to project forward in time. I may decide to sign a group now, but their record may not come out for a few more months or a year or more. If your decisions are based only on yesterday and today, you'll be out-of-date when your records are released. Your job is to anticipate.
- *Greg Geller, Head of A&R, Epic Records*[1]

As an A&R exec, your job is to sign new artists that will make successful, profitable recordings. According to industry statistics, only 16 percent of all records break even, let alone make a profit. Therefore, you have to be very good at predicting success in order to survive for long in A&R. This pressure for releasing successful

---

[1]from *The Big Time* by Greg Geller.

records can often lead A&R pros to become very conservative in signing new talent. Instead they opt for either a well established artist or a new artist with a well-established "sound."

Once the A&R department has found a group, it becomes time to negotiate a contract with the artist. The Business/Legal Department takes care of this part of the record deal. The Business Affairs Department, as it is also called, is perhaps the most stable professionally. No matter how a record company is doing, it will need its business affairs people to continue negotiating and signing contracts.

Another influence on how a record deal is put together is the personal manager or agent. In most cases it is the manager who sits down with the record company executives to work out a contract. The manager receives a certain percentage of the artist's income for this representation. Often a personal manager will take care of much of the business affairs of an artist.

Some of the largest talent agencies are William Morris, CMA, International Creative Management, and Creative Artists Agency. There are hundreds of other agencies. Some agents go on to become personal managers who represent only a small number of people. When the artist, manager, and the record company (including everyone's legal counsel) are happy about their relationship, the music can begin. At this point, a producer is called in to work with the artist to create the studio recording. Studio engineers and other technicians assist the producer in editing and "mixing" the final recording. The producer can provide a great deal of creative input that will influence the particular style or sound of the recording. The most successful producers are those that enhance the recording in such a way that pleases everyone, including the artist, songwriter, and the consumer.

As with the professionals in A&R, a producer's success is based on the dollars-and-cents results of a released album. However, the rewards can be great when success comes (an album selling one million records or more) because producers may receive royalties from sales that result in hundreds of thousands of dollars.

While the artist and producer are hard at work producing a recording, several other professionals get involved in activities gearing for the release of the new record. Artist relations executives keep track of the artists and make sure that they are happy and productive. Marketing professionals begin the strategy for selling the record, including planning jacket design, advertising, distribution, merchandising, and promotional events. Also involved are the publicists who make sure that the newspaper, magazine, radio, and television critics are aware of the new release.

As the record is being released, the promotion department has a crucial role in making sure that each record is played on all the radio stations. Getting "air play" is the primary sales vehicle for a new release. Therefore, a promotion specialist must be on good terms with the program directors of the local radio stations.

The program director at the radio station has fifteen to twenty promotion people calling him every week. There are about two hundred new singles released every week, and every promotion man is working anywhere from one to five records. Every guy from every company is bombarding the programmer. Perhaps twenty of all those new songs deserve air play. And out of them he must pick one or two or maybe three. As a result, there are a lot of cranky radio people out there who make it very difficult for promotion guys to get through.
    - *Gordon Anderson, Head of Promotion for CBS*[2]

---

[2]from *The Big Time* by Greg Geller.

Program directors are swamped with promotion people each week. While the program director is interested in learning what the new releases are, he or she is more interested in what songs will fit into the station's format. Because of this, the promotion person must know a great deal more about radio than recording: what are the demographics for each radio station in the area? Which new releases will appeal most to each station? Getting air play depends upon knowing what the program director is looking for and why.

Working in the promotion department is a high-risk, high-reward business. A promotion person must spend a great deal of time and money to "wine and dine" the program directors and disc jockeys to encourage them to play their company's records. (Sometimes this practice goes beyond wining and dining -- when money and/or gifts are also given. In the industry this illegal activity is referred to as "payola.") Also, the mentality of a recording company's management is that you can never have enough air time. Therefore, it is difficult to feel that your job has been a success. The high pressure of this job makes longevity in the department unlikely. However, for those who survive, the rewards are great: the salaries are high and promotion into senior management is likely.

The next step to the sale of a record involves the distribution of the product to the retailers. Management in this area involves working with transportation companies, wholesalers, and retailers. Work in distribution requires the ability to work with a diverse group of people, from truckers to store owners.

Finally, it is up to the store owners to keep their collection up-to-date with what is being released and played on the local radio stations. Also, in-store displays and special promotions enhance the record sales.

Music Publishing

It would be difficult to talk about the music business without mentioning the music publisher. The activities of the publisher are closely related to all aspects of the business, especially the financial side. You might ask how a music publisher is different from a record company. In fact, many of the large record companies have publishing divisions. So, what does a publisher do?

Every time a songwriter creates a hit song, he or she reaps the rewards in the form of royalties. Music publishers are often the owners or co-owners (with the songwriter) of the copyright. They literally buy the right to "exploit" the song to various parts of the music industry: record companies, radio stations, television networks, movie studios, ad agencies, etc. In other words, each time a song is used, the songwriter and publisher benefit.

Royalties consist of a percentage of the cost of every record sold (called a mechanical royalty) and every song performed (called a performance royalty.) These royalties usually amount to only a few cents per song, but hit songs are played thousands of times a day across the country.

For example, if you published a song that was recorded on an album by James Taylor, you may get a royalty of 4 cents for each record sold. Each time the song was played on the radio or in performance you would get an additional 2 cents. So, if you start multiplying these pennies by a million seller, including earnings from sales of sheet music of the song, you can see the significant earning potential.

Music publishers are huge companies with thousands of songs in their catalogs. They are also individuals who own only a few songs. Songwriters often act as their own publishers. Some of the larger music publishing companies include Chappell, Warner Brothers, MPL Communications, and MCA.

The challenge for the music publisher is to procure the rights to as many hit songs as possible. This means searching for, signing, and hiring talented writers and then negotiating deals with recording artists (to perform the work) and record companies (to record and distribute the work). When a song hits, the publisher must make sure that all contracts are fulfilled.

Positions with a large music publisher are those of general company executive or administrator taking care of the vast amount of paper work involved in keeping track of a large catalog of songs. Once you have the basic experience and know the publishing business, there may be an opportunity for you to become a professional manager. The manager is the one involved in finding the new talent, much like those working in A&R (see page 46) in a record company. Many managers who have good working relationships with songwriters and performers start their own publishing operations.

You might wonder how it is possible to keep track of all the times a song is used in one form or another. True, it is a difficult task. In response to this mammoth endeavor, licensing agencies exist solely to represent songwriters and publishers to the various buyers. BMI (Broadcast Music Inc.) and ASCAP (American Society of Composers, Authors and Publishers) are the largest organizations of this type. They are non-profit organizations that acquire rights from songwriters and publishers and, in turn, grant licenses to use their entire repertories to various buyers. They then monitor the use of their titles and collect and distribute the earnings. These organizations are also sources of jobs and career information.

Music Radio

Those interested in the music business should consider working in radio as well as for a record company or music publisher. The programming division of a radio station is the best place to be because of the contact with the recording industry and the national radio networks.

Most programming comes from three sources: national network programs, independent production companies, and in-house production. Approximately one-third of the nation's radio stations have a network affiliation with NBC, CBS, ABC or PBS (Public Broadcasting System).

An affiliation with a national network connotes a contractual arrangement to receive national programs during certain parts of the day. A smaller part of the broadcast day is made up of programs supplied by local or national independent producers. The rest of the day is produced in the station itself. Some affiliates produce programming for the national network which is then distributed nationwide.

As mentioned above, the primary contact with the record companies is the program director who is responsible for everything going over the airways. Besides meeting with all the record company representatives, the program director must manage the personnel in his/her department, schedule the broadcast day, deal with budgetary matters and production problems.

The most audible radio job is that of the staff announcer or disc jockey. Beginning announcers read commercials and public service announcements, and introduce programs. With experience, the announcers are given the opportunity to create and choose the content of their own shows. Depending upon the size of the station, announcers may be responsible for operating the studio controls, turntables, tape recorders, and other technical equipment. Excellent announcers establish local, sometimes national reputations and become important figures in the music industry.

Some people get started as continuity writers writing commercials, public service announcements, and station promotional announcements. Sometimes continuity writers create advertising copy for in-house productions.

At large stations, producers and directors have the responsibilities of putting together a show or a series from start to finish. They have the creative input that a disc jockey or program director might have at a smaller station.

In very large stations, a music librarian is hired to keep track of extensive record and tape collections. Some librarians are asked to help select music for shows and to consult with the producers on program notes and content.

The other functions in a radio station have to do with the daily business operations: selling advertising space, managing the technical aspects of the station, and handling the general administration of the station. These functions are crucial to the success of a station, but do not have the same exposure to the music industry as do those in programming. (See the case study that follows and Chapter 5 for more on radio station management.)

Music Television (MTV)

Music Television has been one of the major players in the recent turnaround in the music business. It has given tremendous new exposure to recording artists. Music videos not only allow consumers to hear their favorite artists, but to see them as well. Producing a music video is now nearly as important as producing the original recording itself.

Music Television is the largest distributor of music videos in the country. It is primarily a cable television satellite service that provides continuous music programming to thousands of independent cable TV stations throughout the country. It has, in one way, become another national network like ABC, NBC, CBS and PBS. "Air-play" on MTV assures a national audience. MTV has encouraged competition in the local UHF TV markets and there are now hundreds of music stations.

A Few Words about Classical Music

For those interested primarily in classical music, there are a few important differences from the pop/rock sector. First of all, in recent years, classical music accounted for only four to six percent of total industry sales, compared to the 50+ percent commanded by pop/rock. Also, because of the relatively small sales, many new recordings are done by foreign companies.

Sales of classical LP's, CD's [compact disks] and cassettes are booming these days, boosted by the popular acceptance of the compact disk. But while the United States counts as the leading classical music market -- making up some 40 percent of the worldwide total, by most estimates -- the bulk of the profits are flowing to non-American record companies. The old days are long gone, when American recording giants like RCA and Columbia dominated classical sales, signing up the great conductors, singers, instrumentalists and orchestras to exclusive contracts. Today, Europeans control the classical record business.

*- John Rockwell, **New York Times**, 5/86.*

The major American companies still committed to classical recordings with substantial classical divisions include CBS Masterworks, RCA Red Seal, Nonesuch, and Telarc.

Salary

The stories of high rolling expense accounts and astronomical salaries may give the wrong impression to the neophyte. Salaries at entry level in recording vary tremendously depending upon the size and reputation of the company. Working for a major record company could mean a salary around $20,000. However, at a smaller company salaries could begin in the low teens.

Working for a radio station, an entry-level employee in production or sales might expect $14,000. Sales assistants may get more with commission. As you progress in the industry, however, salaries do improve and become quite respectable.

As with all media positions, you are usually paid what you are worth to the organization. If you show an unusual talent for predicting success, you can pretty much write your own ticket.

Job-Hunting Tips

Research

Using this book's introduction as a guide, start to assemble your "Music Industry Notebook." Read the books mentioned in the following bibliography and start reading the industry magazines, *Billboard*, *Radio and Records*, and *Cash Box*. Industry newspapers such as *Variety*, *Back Stage*, *Rolling Stone*, and *The Hollywood Reporter* will be useful. Also, read related trade magazines for different perspectives on the industry. You would be surprised how much information can be culled from publications like *Forbes, Fortune, Advertising Age,* and *Broadcasting.*

Use *Spot Radio, Billboard's International Buyers Guide,* and the *Cash Box Annual Worldwide Directory* as sources to build your target list of employers. Talent agencies are listed in *The International Motion Picture Almanac.*

Write to the major industry associations for information about careers. Also, start compiling your list of personal, alumni, or campus contacts in the recording industry.

Become an expert on your favorite type of music. Your knowledge of a particular genre will be more important than your college degree in many cases. In order to sound committed to a career in music you must know music. This is the fun part, however, so you shouldn't even have to think much about this piece of advice.

Getting Experience

Join your campus radio station. There is no better training ground during your undergraduate years. Record company reps visit college stations on a regular basis to promote new recordings and artists. If you are the program director or a D.J. responsible for your own show, you may get the opportunity to meet with the record company reps. These people should become the first names on your list of future contacts. Also, be sure to keep the outline for and a sample tape of any programming you create.

Become a part of any effort to bring recording artists on campus, either for concerts, workshops, or lectures. Volunteer to do some work for the Office of the Arts, which is often responsible for bringing such people on campus.

Do an unpaid internship at a local radio station that plays the type of music you enjoy. Learn as much as possible about how programming works in a professional radio station. Get to know the program director and D.J.'s and ask how they got started. Add the names of these people to your growing contact list.

Look into the possibility of doing work for a local recording studio. This will give you firsthand experience in the production end of the music business. Consult the directories mentioned before and the local yellow pages.

Write to managers or agencies to set up a summer internship. Consult the directories for lists. Make yourself a good candidate by attending local concerts. Assess who you think the new talent is in your area and be prepared to discuss why. You may just find yourself acting as a local talent scout.

Get a part-time job in a record store. Having a firsthand knowledge of what sells and how fast will come in handy when writing cover letters and during interviews. Try the record and tape wholesalers (distributors, one-stop rack jobbers, importers and exporters). A list is in the *Billboard Directory*.

Speaking of *Billboard*, make a list of all the music trade and consumer magazines. Use your writing skills to work your way into the business by getting a job as a writer or editor. (See Chapter 6) *Rolling Stone*, for example, offers internships year-round for those interested in entertainment journalism.

Contact all the major record companies and inquire about part-time, fill-in, or summer clerical jobs. Any experience inside a major company will be valuable because you will not only get a sense for how the organization is set up, but you may also meet people who can provide invaluable information about industry trends, career histories, and job opportunities.

Entry Points and Strategies

As you might suspect from the discussion above, there are many facets to the music business and, therefore, many possible routes to a career. Begin by determining which of the jobs mentioned above seems most interesting and direct your initial job hunt in that area.

Create a resume that clearly expresses your interest and experience in music. Keep the resume concise and no longer than one page.

Put most of your creative energies into writing a dynamic cover letter. Your goal in the cover letter is to impress the record company or radio station executive with your commitment, drive, potential, and talent. That person should want to meet you after reading your letter. Indicate your ultimate goal, but also a willingness to start at the bottom. End the letter by stating your next move: a follow-up phone call to arrange an appointment. If you have written a successful letter, you should end up with quite a few appointments.

If nothing happens with your initial efforts, expand your search to the peripheral areas. Because there is no formal structure to the music business, getting started anywhere will leave open endless possibilities. However, keep in mind that the major centers in the music business are New York, Los Angeles, and Nashville. Job hunting in these locations will greatly improve your chances of finding work.

Those interested in pursuing a career in classical

music should consider the arts management positions in orchestras and music festivals. Once involved on the inside of the classical music world, it is much easier to learn about how recording contracts are negotiated.

Graduate School

There are a few graduate programs that introduce students to the mechanics of the radio and recording industries. The best programs are associated with the top music schools. However, a graduate degree is not necessary for a successful career in the record business, nor does it guarantee a job in the industry. So, think carefully about investing in this type of education.

Two other types of degree programs are worth thinking about more seriously, however. Because so much importance is placed on the contractual agreement between the artist and the record company, the legal department plays a crucial role. Therefore, one route into the industry is to study law and focus on entertainment law. Try to spend your law school summers in firms that practice this type of law. You will be spending most of your time in the business as a legal advisor and counsel; however, there is always the possibility of branching into other parts of the business.

Pursuing an MBA may lead to a career in the Business Affairs department of a record company. Again, most of your time will be involved crunching numbers and working on spread sheets. However, your talents may be recognized in other areas if you make your interests known.

Case Study

Mary Elizabeth McNary, Public Affairs Officer

Elizabeth works in the public affairs division of ASCAP (The American Society of Composers, Authors and Publishers). ASCAP is America's oldest and most powerful performance rights society. The society handles the royalties of composers from Leonard Bernstein to Madonna, from Stevie Wonder to Johnny Mercer. She is currently working on ASCAP's grassroots lobbying efforts.

I graduated from Harvard/Radcliffe in 1982 with a degree in Romance Languages and Literatures, a Rotary Foundation Fellowship to study music in Rio de Janeiro, and no earthly idea what I wanted to be when I grew up. I had chosen my field of concentration because it had the fewest requirements of any of a myriad of majors in which I was interested. All my life, people older and wiser than myself had told me to keep my options open at all costs. I obliged them, and sampled, with wild abandon, ethics, art history, economics, astronomy, creative writing, East Asian history, and computer science.

The only area outside my field of concentration that I explored with a modicum of logic was music. I took music courses and sang with choral groups throughout my Harvard career (except for the first semester of my freshman year, when I rowed crew. I was keeping my options open, okay?). I toured Europe with the Harvard/ Radcliffe Collegium Musicum, traveled to Bermuda with the Radcliffe Pitches, perfected my Portuguese by singing bossa nova with my roommate at coffee houses around campus, and pleased my family to no end by regularly performing Irish rebel songs with a guitar-playing boyfriend of similar family heritage.

After graduation, with a year and a half to fill before

going off to Rio on scholarship, I took a job as a paralegal in Manhattan. Paralegal departments in New York law firms are watering holes for Ivy-League grads who can't type and don't know whether or not they want to go to law school. I learned that I did not. I also honed my writing and editorial skills. Writing is the most important part of my job here at ASCAP, so my time was well spent.

I left the law firm, went to Rio, immersed myself in Brazil's wonderful music, did some dinner theater, and traveled throughout the country. A year later, I came home very tan and very worried about what would happen next. I had dutifully kept my options open for twenty-five years, and suddenly it was time to enter Adult Life. I still hadn't the foggiest notion of what I wanted to do, so I took those interest tests in which they match your likes and dislikes with those of professionals from a variety of fields. According to those tests, I would have been happiest as a clergywoman. Unfortunately, that was one option not open to me as a Roman Catholic.

An aunt of mine, who is a headhunter, prescribed a book that changed my life by changing my attitude about work. Tom Jackson's *Guerrilla Tactics in the Job Market* convinced me that choosing a field would not jeopardize my precious options at all. Rather, I would be electing to exercise the most appealing option. What a relief! I opted for a job in the music industry, and set about getting one.

For the next year and a half, I lived at home with my family. I supported myself by doing freelance editorial work, and devoted every spare minute to learning about my chosen field. I poured over the trade journals, wrote letters, made cold calls, and talked to everyone I could think of who was even remotely involved with music. I routinely worked 60-hour weeks for 20-hour pay. Without the help and support of family and friends, I never would have reached my goal.

At first, I thought that I might like to be a radio announcer. I knew nothing about broadcasting, but I had a solid knowledge of both popular and classical music. With a command of several foreign languages, I was confident that I could pronounce any difficult name or musical term that they threw at me. I wrote to all my favorite deejays and spent a shift in the studio with each of them. All were happy to answer my questions and to make suggestions about how to break in to radio. None suggested going to broadcasting school; all suggested doing an internship.

I researched internships at Harvard's Office of Career Services, and landed one at WMRE, a 15,000 watt A.M. station in the throes of a bankruptcy proceeding. I volunteered to work two days a week writing copy for their evening magazine show. Within a couple of months, I had my own program, affectionately known as Hoppin' in the Hub: Where we give you an insider's view of the Boston music scene. Hoppin' was a live weekly show that I produced and co-hosted with another intern. We interviewed local and national musicians, playing their records and hosting their live studio performances. Working on Hoppin' put me in touch with musicians, publicists, promoters, and club owners, and gave me more ideas (more options!) about careers in music. It also gave me access to a radio production studio, in which I acquired some technical skills.

During one of my early visits with a disc jockey at WBOS in Boston, I met a young announcer who had gone to Harvard. He had run the soundboard for a musical that I had done as an undergraduate, and he recognized me as I was touring the station. He took me under his wing, and taught me everything I ever wanted to know about radio production. He also listened regularly to Hoppin' in the Hub and critiqued it. When an early-morning soundboard operator's job opened up some months later at this station, he saw that I got it, and trained me to do it.

I worked Sundays from six in the morning until noon airing public-service and syndicated "countdown" shows. Thanks to my knowledge of foreign languages and classical music, I also got myself hired to do a Saturday night shift at WCRB. I soon discovered that I was not cut out to jock concert music. I did not like the erratic pace of classical announcing, and I was an abysmal failure at it.

While I was failing at WCRB, I did an internship in the national promotions department of the Rounder Records Group, a Cambridge indie (that's industry jargon for "independent record company") with a good catalogue of folk and new acoustic music. I tracked the press coverage, airplay, and record sales of Rounder artists on a computer with industry-specific software. (Boy, was I ever glad that I had kept that computer-science option open when I was at Harvard!) I read everything that I could get my hands on about the record industry, asked tons of questions, and copied hundreds of names and numbers out of my supervisor's Rollodex.

While I was juggling the Rounder job, my freelance work, and the weekend shifts at 'CRB and 'BOS, the Promotions Director at WBOS went to Australia for a month to catch the America's Cup. Suddenly, I was Acting Promotions Director. I did everything from dressing up as a pumpkin and distributing balloons at a Fall Harvestfest that the station sponsored to supervising a post World Series autograph session with the Red Sox. It was great!

I had a lot of fun while I was exploring and learning, but I didn't get much sleep and I never had any money. There came a time when I started to panic. It seemed that, despite a year and a half of enriching experiences, I was not much closer to landing a permanent job in the music industry than I had been when I'd picked the field in the first place. I still wasn't exactly sure what I wanted to do within the music business, and I didn't know where to turn for guidance. The one who finally shamed me into figuring out what to do was my mother! One day I was lamenting my fate to my mother, who had ever so subtly plastered the refrigerator door with fliers advertising a symposium on careers in investment banking. "Why on earth," I whined, "do they insist on holding all these programs about how to get into fields that everybody knows how to get into?! You wanna be a banker, you do a training program for two years and then go to business school. You wanna be a lawyer, you survive the paralegal experience and move on to law school. "Why," I yelled, my fury mounting, "doesn't somebody put together a conference on how to get a job in the music business for a change?"

"Why don't you?" my mother asked quietly. I had no choice but to do so. I rose to her challenge, and designed, budgeted, planned, coordinated, managed, and hosted Harvard's first conference on behind-the-scenes jobs in the music business. The program was funded by the offices of Deans Archie Epps and Philippa Bovet, as well as by Radcliffe Career Services and Harvard's OCS. I invited music industry professionals from a wide variety of fields to participate in a panel discussion and networking party. Everybody gets a kick out of being invited to speak at Harvard and all the people whose brains I had been dying to pick were happy to participate.

Of course, I called every alum who had anything at all to do with music before I invited people to speak at the conference. One alum, who is a career advisor at the career services office, was helpful beyond belief. He referred me to some fine speakers, who in turn put me in touch with their contacts. Music is a very cliquey business, and the best thing to do is to get to know the movers and shakers. With the Harvard name behind me, I found that task to be fairly easy.

The conference was a big success. I hopped the plane to New York the very next day, and arranged to meet with the speakers whose professions most interested me. I asked them to review my resume and tell me what it lacked. Here at ASCAP, the gentleman who had been on my panel in Cambridge, took one look and said, "Um, Elizabeth, I would encourage you to talk with our Public Affairs Department." Three weeks later, I had a job.

The best advice that I ever received came from a dear friend who is a technician for a Boston-area television station. He told me to remember that I was smart, that I was capable, and that there is no such thing as unrelated experience. So do keep your options open. Do explore ethics and micro-biology and Zen. Do make the most of your liberal education. And once you choose the Chosen Field, don't ever be afraid to ask a stupid question about it. Be tireless in your pursuit of information and unrelenting in your campaign to make that information work for you. At the risk of sounding like the clergywoman that I don't have the option of becoming, *Deus vobiscum* on your way!

Bibliography

Books

Career Opportunities in the Music Industry, Shelly Field, Facts on File, New York, New York, 1986.
Contains useful general information about the field. Excellent job descriptions of 79 positions in the industry, each including a detailed outline of the job, career ladder, salary, employment/advancement prospects.

Careers in Radio, National Association of Broadcasters, Washington, D.C., 1976.
Basic description of jobs in radio.

Creative Careers, Gary Blake and Robert Bly, Wiley Press, New York, 1983.
Excellent descriptive and insightful chapter on the music business. Very good bibliography.

Inside Track, Ross and Kathryn Petras, Vintage Books, New York, 1986.
Focuses on individual companies, some in the entertainment business, including A&M Records and Warner Records.

The Music/Record Career Handbook, Joseph Csida, Billboard Publications Inc., New York, New York, 1975.
Somewhat dated, but still a surprisingly accurate account of finding work in the music business. Largely a personal account from the author's perspective. However, a good source of cultural information and general career information.

This Business of Music, Sidney Shemel and M. William Krasilovsky, Billboard Publications, Inc., New York, New York, 1985.
A handbook on the strictly business and legal side

of the music business. The information is very detailed and technical, but it is a good introduction to some important aspects of the music industry.

Directories

1989 Internships, F&W Publications, Cincinnati, Ohio, annual.
Describes internships and summer jobs in radio and music, along with other categories. Eligibility and application information for each listing.

Billboard's International Buyer's Guide, Billboard Publications, Inc., New York, New York, annual.
The yearly source of information about the recording industry. Comprehensive listings of record companies, industry statistics, music publishers, wholesalers, etc. Refer to this directory for your list making.

Getting Work Experience, Betsy Bauer, Dell Publishing, New York, New York, 1985.
Among other listings, describes summer internship programs in radio. Gives pertinent application information including pay scale (if any), qualifications desired, and deadlines.

International Motion Picture Almanac, Quigley Publishing Company, New York, annual.
Contains primarily information on motion picture industry, but has a great list of talent agents.

Spot Radio, Standard Rate & Data Service, Wilmette, Illinois, monthly.
Technical and detailed information on all major radio stations in the United States. Lists essential information, including address, phone, format, and list of key personnel for each station. Good source for making prospect list.

Periodicals

Billboard, Billboard Publications, Inc., New York, New York, weekly.
The music industry trade magazine. Learn the ins-and-outs of the business, including who and what is "top 40."

Variety, Variety, Inc., New York, New York, daily in New York and Los Angeles, otherwise weekly. The entertainment industry's trade magazine.

Chapter 3

Newspapers & News Magazines

To call working for newspapers a way of life instead of simply a career goes to the heart of what journalism is all about. It implies not only a commitment, the kind that would be required for going into the other professions, but a willingness to become a particular kind of person, one who becomes a trained observer of human events rather than a direct participant in them.

-John Tebbel, writer, former New York Times staff writer[1]

Industry Profile

In many ways journalism is the perfect career for the liberal arts graduate. It allows you to examine a wide variety of topics, to study and analyze them, and then to write about them. Sounds like the outline for most of your courses, right? Naturally, this is a simplistic description; however, ideally a journalist does proceed as outlined above.

On the surface journalism can appear to be an exciting and honorable profession. The activities involved in reporting the news, informing the public, being the "watchdog" for society encourage a romantic impression. However, work in journalism, while it contains many of the elements just described, also includes the usual amount of routine and boring assignments. Going from president of the campus paper to beat reporter at a small city paper can be a shock.

---

[1]from *Opportunities in Publishing Careers*
by John Tebbel

As for the health of the medium itself, the newspaper business is alive, but how well it is depends upon whom you consult. The Dow Jones Newspaper Fund, in its *Journalism Career and Scholarship Guide*, states that: "the message is simple. The newspaper industry is very healthy and continues to make enormous profits ... The future is bright and exciting." Others state that more and more papers are going out of business every year, the general populace is becoming illiterate, and who knows what the future brings.

Perhaps a more realistic view of the industry comes from *Editor and Publisher*, the industry's trade magazine. In 1985 there were 1,676 daily newspapers in the United States; this reflects seven new papers and nineteen that closed operations. In 1985, daily circulation of these papers totaled nearly 63,000,000. This reflects a general upturn in the previous four years. Looking at the figures, it would seem safe to say that the industry will survive for many years to come.

The scope of print journalism runs the range from large daily metropolitan dailies, to national news magazines, to small-town weeklies, to the freelance reporter or stringer. Wire services and large syndicates make up another facet of the industry. Also, newspaper groups (corporations owning many newspapers in different cities) are growing.

Career Profiles

Newspapers

There are many jobs on a newspaper: production, advertising, promotion, circulation, photography, graphic design, and computer technology, as well as writing, editing, and reporting. This chapter will focus on the reporting and editing jobs.

Although many editors of large dailies began their careers as "copy boys," that entry point is no longer prescribed (although still possible at *The New York Times*). General assignment reporter is a more typical entry-level job for this track. The general assignment reporter collects news through interviews and research, or from the wire services.

The day is often spent reading mail -- news releases, government reports, suggestions for stories -- and talking on the phone -- answering calls and calling people for interviews. A general assignment reporter is usually responsible for writing his or her own articles which will be edited and turned back for reworking. On occasion, under deadline pressure, a reporter will phone in a story to the editor.

A beat reporter is an entry-level job with different elements from those of the general assignment reporter. A reporter's "beat" may be city hall, the municipal court, or the police station. On these beats a reporter is expected to learn the nuts and bolts of the particular organization: Where does it maintain its records? Who is the best, most reliable source of information? Who is the most willing to talk? The beat reporter will usually call in stories to the rewrite editor.

Sometimes, especially on smaller city dailies, a general assignment reporter will also be assigned as the rewrite editor. Rewrite editors, with headphones in place, often write the story as they listen to the beat reporter's account. On a small paper, a staff member may have both editing and reporting duties because of the short supply of staff members.

City editors organize the newsroom. They are responsible for getting in all the stories and photos by deadline. A city editor may have several assistants, depending upon the size of the paper. Editors are responsible, too, for the initial approval of a reporter's story and sending it along to the copy desk.

Once a reporter's story is approved, the copy editors take over and check the article for spelling, punctuation, and usage. They also mark the copy (article) for the printers, if necessary. Most larger papers now are computerized so that "marking copy" is done on a computer terminal.

Once the raw editing is completed, the copy editor will write the headline for the article. All news stories pass through the copy desk before appearing in print. Because of this, copy editors are in a good position to learn quickly about different writing and reporting styles.

There is no prescribed career path for journalists. Many prefer reporting and move up the career ladder, possibly from general assignment reporter to specialist reporter to bureau reporter to foreign correspondent or syndicated columnist. Some reporters make the switch to editing by displaying an aptitude and letting the management know they are interested.

The career path of an editor might lead through the various jobs of copy editor, assistant city editor, telegraph editor, cable editor, news editor, night editor, managing editor, associate editor, and editor-in-chief. The editors determine the content of the newspaper by assigning stories to reporters and selecting the stories to be printed.

Wire Services

The wire services provide news to newspapers, radio and television stations throughout the United States and the world. With their hundreds of bureaus, they can cover news in a certain locality for people far from the scene. The news services deliver "packages" to other news outlets via their sports, business and news wires. The three major wire services are the Associated Press, United Press International, and Reuters.

The wire services generally prefer to hire people who have had two years newspaper experience, but they will occasionally take people straight from college. Those who begin with the wire services will get a crash course in the fundamentals of editing and reporting and an immediate chance to cover good stories. Compared to newspapers, wire services have more deadline pressure, as well as a demand for great volume.

A reporter usually begins as a general news reporter before specializing. The work day is spent taking stories on the phone, fact checking, covering outside assignments, writing, rewriting, editing, and initiating or channeling the news. The career path for a wire service reporter might lead to top coverage of national news.

In many ways, the life of a wire service reporter is like that of a reporter on a major daily paper. One major difference, however, is that wire service reporters do not get by-line credit. Every reporter at a wire service has the same by-line: the name of his or her service. This anonymity may not appeal to many journalists.

Even though wire services look for experience they also depend upon stringers for much of the late-breaking news. Stringers are freelance reporters who are close to the scene of a story or who develop their own story ideas. Stringing is one way for people who have little journalism experience to build a collection of clips (writing samples).

A would-be journalist can begin stringing in college for a major paper or news magazine by covering the stories coming from the college community. Once out of college, stringers often are people in other professions who can write insightfully about their own specialty or area of expertise. It is difficult, however, to begin your career working solely as a stringer because of the unpredictable number of assignments.

For those with an interest in becoming foreign correspondents, working for a wire service might be a good starting place. There is more mobility in wire services than in any other part of the news business. The opportunity to be assigned to a foreign bureau of a wire service is much greater than at a conventional newspaper or news magazine.

One other way to become a foreign correspondent is as a stringer. If you happen to be travelling or visiting another country, you might be in a very good locale to cover any unusual news. It becomes a matter of establishing contact with the appropriate wire service bureau chief. Of course, excellent foreign language skills and extensive travel experience make the you a much stronger candidate for the job of foreign correspondent.

News Magazines

News magazines represent an important news outlet which many people read for coverage of current national and international issues. The major difference among the different print media is the timeliness of the news reported. Those working at a news magazine may not be able to report the latest news, but they do have the opportunity to cover news in greater depth than the wire services and dailies.

Some of the major news magazines include *Time*, *Life*, *Newsweek*, *The Nation*, *The New Republic*, *U.S. News &*

World Report, and *Foreign Policy.* Editors, staff writers, researchers, and reporters at domestic and foreign bureaus all have a part in gathering and disseminating the news. Editorial and staff writing jobs go to people with years of experience at either the same magazine or another publication. The reporting jobs are also extremely competitive, usually requiring several years of previous reporting experience on a major publication, such as a large metropolitan daily.

There are entry-level jobs as researchers at these publications. The researchers are primarily responsible for background research and fact checking. A major publication might have as many as 35 researchers, with two or three openings a year. They generally look for people with a demonstrated interest in journalism -- either a journalism degree, work experience on a college newspaper, a news internship or stringing experience.

Salary

Starting salaries for entry-level reporters vary from paper to paper. If you are working for a paper that is part of a newspaper group, you can expect slightly better salary ($300 to $450 per week). Those working for smaller, independent papers or magazines usually receive less (from $200 per week up). Salaries improve, but are never outstanding compared to other fields within mass media. A full-fledged reporter at a 100,000 circulation daily might only make $30 to $40,000 per year. It is clear that you should not go into journalism for the money.

Job-Hunting Tips

According to a 1985 industry poll of 28 percent of daily newspapers from across the U.S., 25.1 percent of all newly hired journalists came directly from college in 1985. Of the college grads, 85 percent were journalism majors. An estimated 5000 jobs come open for college grads. Twenty-thousand people graduate with journalism degrees each year. For the liberal arts graduate, this indicates pretty stiff competition.

However, don't let the numbers discourage you. In the long run, having a good liberal arts education gives a journalist a tremendous career advantage. It provides the kind of broad background necessary to keep a career active and growing. Many journalists "burn out" because they view their profession simply as a craft and not as an intellectual pursuit.

Getting Experience

In order to compete with all the journalism graduates you must be well prepared. Newspaper editors are looking for young journalists who can fit right into their organizations without much training. They are looking for people who can cover a story well and write the facts in clear, straightforward prose. The ability to write a good "hard-news" story is greatly valued by most city editors.

Therefore, make sure that you get experience writing this type of story. Join one of your campus publications. Collect ten or fifteen articles that show your basic writing talent. Feature stories and reviews may be more fun to write, but be sure to have examples of your ability to write the simple news stories, too.

Summer internships are an excellent means of broadening your experience. Most newspapers have some sort of program. Underclassmen should concentrate on their local hometown papers in freshman and sophomore years. Juniors are eligible for internships at the major papers and news magazines. Deadlines for these internships begin in late November. Consult *The Student Guide to Mass Media Internships* for a comprehensive listing of hundreds of internships around the country. Writer's Digest Books publishes a similar, more general guide on internships. Another publication entitled *Getting Work Experience* will add possibilities to your list. An excellent new publication is the *Newspaper Career Directory,* which lists internships and training programs, among other useful information.

If working for a campus publication is not for you, become a campus stringer for a major magazine or newspaper. Once you have an idea for an article, send a query letter to the managing editor of your target publication. A query letter should be approximately one page in length and should state clearly your idea and how you plan to research it. It should also elaborate on any relevant background you may have for writing the article. Be sure you have the appropriate editor's name.

Follow your letter with a phone call about one week after mailing it. It is possible that the editor may take the article "on speculation," accepting it only after it's written and up to standards. Some editors will work with a stringer on an article and help to develop it. The key to getting published is to know the publication; be sure to read several issues so you are familiar with the type of stories that are published.

Stringing is also the obvious route to follow for those who have decided near the end of their college careers, or even after college that journalism is the career they want to pursue. If the decision is made after college, the strategy usually includes working two jobs at once: one job to pay the rent and the other as a stringer developing your writing. Many successful journalists have begun careers this way, so don't assume that work on a campus publication is a prerequisite.

The essential experience, no matter where you get it, is writing. You will be judged primarily on how well you write a story and how you show the confidence needed to deal with the pressure of daily deadlines. After you have examples of your writing in hand, you can then begin the arduous task of finding a job.

Getting the Job

Editor and Publisher Yearbook, The Magazine Industry Marketplace, The Writer's Market, and *The Gale Directory of Publications* are good sources for your target list of employers. Because there are so many publications throughout the country, it may be wise to concentrate on particular parts of the country to conduct your job search.

When compiling your list, keep in mind that most major metropolitan dailies require two to five years of full-time reporting experience on another paper for their entry-level reporting jobs. Smaller papers are excellent places to learn and should be looked on as a springboards and not as traps. They offer the opportunity to learn various aspects of the trade quickly.

Once you have a preliminary list compiled, begin putting together a list of potential career advisers. The alumni contacts in journalism are excellent. They can often give you a list of four or five top-notch small dailies or weeklies that would be good starting places. Show them your list for their insight and suggestions. Show the advisers your writing samples and ask for suggestions about which to include with your resume and job letter.

Before you start sending out letters be aware that very few employers will be willing to reimburse you for travelling expenses. Send out letters to employers who are in the same region of the country so that you are not wasting time and money making long trips for a single interview.

Your letter should be brief and straightforward (just

like the news stories you will be writing). This does not mean that you can send a form letter. Individualize each letter and address it to the managing editor. If you must, call the paper to get the correct name. If you are familiar with the paper, mention it in the letter. The letter should outline your writing experience and any particularly important stories you may have written. Mention that you are confident that you can become productive quickly once you begin work.

Your resume should be one page and easy to read. Make your journalism experience stand out clearly. In each description, list first the names of the different publications where you have worked. When the editor is reading the resume, your commitment and experience should be obvious.

With your letter and resume, include 6 to 10 of your best writing samples or "clips." Make reproductions of your clips so that they fit neatly on letter-sized paper and are easy to read. It is perfectly acceptable to cut and paste so that your stories fit nicely in this format. Be sure to include the publication's masthead and date.

Once your job-hunting packet is ready, you can begin your mailing. It is greatly to your advantage to follow the mailing with a personal visit. Positive responses to your mailing may ask you to stop by if you are in the area. You really cannot expect much more from a response, and you must take the initiative.

Respond to every positive or even semi-positive response. If you can't go to interview immediately, send more clips. You absolutely must be persistent. Visit the same papers more than once and try to develop personal contacts in the newsrooms. If you don't have the energy to do a good, thorough job hunt, you may not have the energy to be a journalist.

When you get an offer, evaluate it in terms of the

hard news reporting experience you will gain. You may have some less-than-glamorous duties to begin with, and you may be located in the sticks, but if you get some good experience, you will be able to move up quickly. Also, consult some of the advisers who helped you along the way. Work hard at the first job, make a name for yourself, and you'll find that career advancement will come quite naturally.

Case Study

Ron Roach, Reporter

*Ron Roach had an active interest in politics as an undergraduate and concentrated in government. During his freshman year he wrote for the **Harvard Political Review** and went on to a summer internships with the **Wilson Quarterly** and **Newsweek**. He is now a staff writer at the **Roanoke News**.*

When it came time for me to decide what I was going to do after college, I chose journalism because I wanted to combine my interests in writing and public service. When I entered Harvard in the fall of 1981, I had planned to study electrical engineering. My interests, however, shifted to government, and I decided that I would eventually go to law school. I had vague, undefined interests about becoming a lawyer, but I was certain that I wanted to study government. I also wanted to write and I ended up joining the *Harvard Political Review* the spring of my freshman year.

Not until fall of my senior year did I decide to commit myself to finding a job in journalism. It had taken some time because when I started out writing articles for the *Harvard Political Review*, I knew very little about journalism. I was fortunate because I later got good summer jobs where I learned more about the profession.

The summer after sophomore year, I landed a writing internship at the *Wilson Quarterly* magazine in Washington. My editor was a former newspaper correspondent who had worked at the *Washington Post* and *The New York Times*. He made it a point to encourage my fellow interns and me to pursue journalism as a career. After my junior year, I worked as an intern in the Atlanta bureau of *Newsweek*. The high-powered world of the national weekly news magazine was a seductive one. I had enjoyed working in Atlanta because I got a chance to travel all over Georgia and covered a variety of stories that took place throughout the South.

When I got back to Harvard, I decided to look for a job at daily newspapers. It was in daily newspaper journalism where I realized I would have to pay my dues and get valuable experience. I also figured that I would make a two-to-three year commitment before deciding whether I would stick with journalism. If I stayed in the profession, I believed I would eventually go to a *Newsweek* or *Time* or become a national correspondent for a major newspaper. If I didn't, I would get another job or go to graduate school.

That fall, I sent my resume and my writing clips to newspapers all over the East Coast. Being from High Point, North Carolina, I didn't want to stray too far west or northwest. I had liked Washington and Atlanta very much when I worked in those cities, and wanted most to start out in those places. I applied to publications such as the *Charlotte Observer*, the *Washington Post*, the *Wall Street Journal*, the *Richmond Times-Dispatch*, *Newsweek*, the *Raleigh News and Observer*, the *Hartford Courant*, the *Providence Journal*, the *Virginian Pilot-Ledger Star*, and the *Atlanta Journal-Constitution*.

Unfortunately, my lack of newspaper writing experience made it difficult for editors to be encouraging about job prospects even though I had applied to their internship programs. I had hoped that getting an internship would inevitably lead to getting a regular staff job.

In addition to looking for a job, I stayed quite busy organizing the Harvard Black Film Society. I had started the society with the intention of reviving the Harvard Black Independent Film Festival. I probably could have made the job search a little easier had I completed a *Harvard Crimson* tryout that I began in the fall, but I dropped it to concentrate on the film festival. Besides the film festival and the half-completed tryout, I was editing articles for the *Harvard Political Review*, stringing for *Newsweek on Campus* magazine, and taking a demanding Expos 2 course. I was not writing a senior thesis.

By March, the month of the film festival, I had yet to find a job or internship and I began to worry a little. If I didn't get one of the newspaper jobs I wanted, I would settle on working for the Massachusetts state government because I had a good friend who was a state administrator, or I would go to a small urban weekly newspaper.

But good fortune prevailed once again. A week before spring break, the managing editor of the *Roanoke Times & World News* in Roanoke, Virginia, called me to ask if I would be interested in an internship at his newspaper. I don't recall ever having heard of his paper, although Roanoke was 100 miles directly north of my hometown. The editor of the *Roanoke Times & World News* told me he had learned that I was looking for an internship from an editor at the *Virginian Pilot-Ledger Star* in Norfolk. It happened that both newspapers are owned by the same company, Landmark Communications. I was invited to Roanoke for an interview that was scheduled during spring break.

Before going to Roanoke, I tried hard to remember what the city was like from the few times I had passed through as a child. A brochure about the *RT&WN* sent to me by the managing editor was more useful than my memory. I learned that Roanoke, a city of 107,000, was located in a valley surrounded by the Blue Ridge Mountains in Southwest Virginia. The Roanoke Valley's metropolitan area has a population of 220,000 and the newspaper's circulation area has about one million. The newspaper's weekday circulation is 125,000 and 130,000 on Sundays. Those figures reassured me that I wasn't heading to any isolated outpost. It suited me fine that my parents' home was a two-hour drive; Richmond was three hours away, and Washington was a four-hour trip.

After my interview, I was offered an internship with the possibility of getting a full-time staff position upon successful completion of the internship. I accepted the offer and four days after graduating with the Class of 1985, I reported to work.

The internship went well for me and I was offered a job in August. Since then, I have been working mostly as a general assignment reporter with some business reporting responsibilities. In March 1986, I was assigned to cover Patrick and Henry counties, and the town of Vinton.

My experience in Roanoke has been a good one. I have been learning journalism from the bottom up. I have covered traffic accidents, murder trials, zoning hearings, town council meetings, a House Congressional race, state government officials, and much more. My advice to aspiring journalists who are still in college is that you should get all the experience you possibly can writing for a newspaper. You should write for community papers as well as campus publications. Editors are most interested in seeing that you know how to write for a newspaper.

Luck was good to me, but getting experience is always better.

Bibliography

Books

Headlines and Deadlines, Robert Garst and Theodore Bernstein, Columbia University Press, New York, New York, 1982.
A manual for copy editors. Teaches some of the basics of editing copy and writing headlines. Useful information to help prepare for any copy editing tests you may have to take in the job-hunting process.

Inside Track, Ross and Kathryn Petras, Vintage Books, New York, 1986.
Focuses on individual companies, some in journalism, including the Los Angeles Times, the New York Times, the Wall Street Journal and Time.

Investigative Reporting and Editing, Paul N. Williams, Prentice Hall, Englewood Cliffs, New Jersey, 1978.
A basic textbook on investigative reporting, what it is, how it's done, and what the issues are. Good background material.

Opportunities in Journalism, John Tebbel, VGM Career Horizons, Skokie, Illinois, 1982.
A good overview of the possibilities within the field. An excellent place to start background research.

Directories

1989 Internships, F&W Publications, Cincinnati, Ohio, annual.
Describes internships and summer jobs in newspapers and magazines, along with other categories. Eligibility and application information for each listing.

The Editor & Publisher Yearbook, Editor & Publisher Co., New York, New York, annual.
The source for information about newspapers. For daily papers around the country, lists a wealth of information, including the basics and the names of the editors of all major sections of each paper. Also, has a list of the top 100 daily papers by circulation.

Getting Work Experience, Betsy Bauer, Dell Publishing, New York, New York, 1985.
Among other listings, describes summer internship programs in print journalism. Gives pertinent application information including pay scales (if any), qualifications desired, and deadlines.

The Gale Directory of Publications, IMS Press, Fort Washington, Pennsylvania, annual.
The most comprehensive directory of newspapers, magazines, journals, and newsletters. Organized geographically by city and state with useful subject indexes.
Gives only very basic information, however. Use this directory to compile a comprehensive list.
Journalism Career and Scholarship Guide, Dow Jones Newspaper Fund, Princeton, New Jersey, annual.
Valuable guide to basic career information and graduate school information.

New England Media Directory, Burrelle's Media Directories, Livingston, New Jersey, annual.
Listing of all media sources in the New England area, including addresses, phone numbers, and key personnel of daily and weekly papers and magazines.

New York Media Directory, Burrelle's Media Directories, Livingston, New Jersey, annual.
Listing of all media sources in New York, including addresses, phone, and key personnel of daily and weekly papers and magazines.

The Newspaper Career Directory, Career Publishing , Inc., New York, New York, annual. One of the best sources of general career information. Has articles by industry professionals, a job-hunting section, and listings of internships and training programs.

The Student Guide to Mass Media Internships, Vol. 1, Ronald Claxton, Intern Research Group, University of Colorado, Boulder, Colorado, annual.

List internships available in daily and weekly newspapers and a limited number of magazines with requirements, pay scales, and deadlines.

Periodicals

Editor & Publisher, Editor & Publisher Co., New York, New York, weekly.

Chapter 4

Broadcast Journalism

You have to be a quick study . . . premium is placed on quick analytic skills. You can get a research file and after an hour reading it, bring yourself up-to-date on a subject. Then you've got to be able to analyze and synthesize the new information and be able to write it very quickly with people breathing down your neck. And that's not everybody's cup of tea.

- Mike Jensen, NBC News
Financial Correspondent

Industry Profile

Unlike print journalism where a single reporter is responsible for a single story, teamwork is the key in broadcast journalism. For every on-the-scene reporter, there are at least a half dozen others involved in getting the story on air. To get an idea of the complex nature of the process, a discussion of how broadcasting is organized is in order.

Network Television and Radio

The three major networks, ABC, CBS, and NBC, supply programming to network-owned or affiliated local stations. The networks are headquartered in New York City and the national television and radio news programs for each network are produced there. The major divisions of one network include: television network; affiliate relations; network and spot sales; advertising and promotion; entertainment; sports; news; owned stations; international television; television planning; broadcast operations and engineering; broadcast standards; merchandising; music; and quality control. Notice how news is sandwiched between many other divisions and departments. All the divisions, however, have some impact on news operations.

There are hundreds of different jobs in these various divisions and to discuss each would take another book. In fact, read *Opportunities in Television and Video* for a breakdown of more than 80 different jobs.

Local Television & Radio Stations

Local stations may be either owned by a network, affiliated with a network, or independent. Independent stations, which do not have access to the programming supplied by the three networks, buy or produce all their own programs, including news. Affiliated stations carry programs supplied by the network during part of the broadcast day and buy or produce their own programs to fill the remainder of the day. Network-owned stations operate much like affiliates, but have the security of being owned by the major network. (FCC regulations limit ownership by any one network to twelve television stations, twelve AM radio stations, and twelve FM radio stations.)

Corporation for Public Broadcasting and Public Broadcasting Services (CPB and PBS)

The Corporation for Public Broadcasting is a non-profit, non-governmental agency which is funded by the government and private sources. Its purpose is to promote and finance the development and sustenance of public radio and television stations, program production centers, and regional networks. It also conducts audience research and studies emerging communications technologies. CPB helped to establish and continues to support the Public Broadcasting Service, the first nation-wide regular interconnection service for public television stations. It does the same for National Public Radio, the primary network of public radio stations.

The Public Broadcasting Service is a non-profit corporation which provides national programming for public television stations. It conducts research on the program needs of local stations, selects programs offered by local public TV stations and independent producers, and distributes the programs through live interconnection and videotape. Funding is provided by CPB. Its full range of services include: national promotion, program acquisition and scheduling, legal services, development and fundraising support, engineering and technical studies, representation before Congress and federal agencies, and research and financial planning. A listing of PBS officers can be found in the Television Factbook, Services Volume.

Local Public Television and Radio Stations

There are approximately 270 non-commercial television stations and 1000 non-commercial radio stations in the United States. Each is involved in producing its own programs as well as those supplied by PBS. Often a local news program, such as Boston WGBH's 10 O'Clock News, will be produced to supplement the nationally distributed *McNeil/Lehrer News Hour.*

Programs produced by local stations are often distributed nationally by PBS, such as WGBH's *Nova.* Ongoing programs are usually produced by a team within the local station. However, most of the special programs and mini-series are produced by independent producers. This keeps costs down. One fact of life about public broadcasting is that it is in constant financial peril.

Cable Television

Cable Television, which transmits signals to homes by means of wire via a shielded cable, was developed in the late 1940's to aid reception in rural areas. A breakthrough in cable television occurred in 1975 when two cable companies began using the RCA satellite Satcom 1 to distribute programming nationally. The industry went through rapid changes in the late 70's and early 80's and continues to change as new technologies for transmitting and receiving signals are developed.

Currently, in addition to improving reception, cable television offers many additional channels that may carry local programs, programs from stations in other cities, or programs from networks which create programs for cable only. These cable networks are competitors of the commercial networks for viewers and have already begun to dramatically effect how people watch television. However, viewers have to pay for the cable service and an additional amount for any special programming.

Subscription Television

The special programming provided by cable networks has spread into all fields. MTV provides music entertainment 24-hours a day. HBO, the oldest network, provides a variety of programming consisting primarily of movies. CNN (Cable News Network) provides continuous news coverage. Until very recently the edge cable networks had on ABC, NBC, and CBS was the no-commercial format. Viewers seem willing to pay for uninterrupted programming. However, competition within the cable industry has lead some of the leading cable networks to introduce limited advertising. Employment opportunities in cable, once plentiful, are now becoming limited due to a maturing of the industry. In news, the opportunities come primarily from CNN and a few new start-ups.

Local Cable Stations

Many of the newer cable stations have production

facilities to produce local programs and to provide public access. These facilities are provided, in most cases, because of the franchise agreement between the particular town and a cable company. The franchise agreement usually requires the cable station to provide several channels for broadcasting coverage of local events such as town meetings, high school athletic events, musical recitals and plays, etc.

Also, the station must allow individuals in the community the opportunity to produce their own programs (public access). Although the quality of programming coming from these local cable stations is usually low, it is a good training ground for would-be producers, directors, and reporters.

Now, Back to the News

As mentioned above, many people are involved in producing a single news story. Also, it is important to note that even the smallest television or radio station is involved in producing news programming. Therefore, opportunities exist all over the country.

All news departments have people to gather news, write and edit the news, and produce the show. In a small news department, one person may have a variety of duties, while in a larger department people have responsibility for specific functions. In most cities, news personnel have multiple duties. The number of straight news writers is diminishing with the increasing number of on-air reporters who write their own scripts. Even at the networks, the anchors are involved in the writing, editing, and production of the program. News directors at many radio stations must gather the news, write the script, edit tape, and broadcast the news themselves.

The entry-level jobs are primarily in reporting and writing, although to get those jobs, beginners often must do a stint as a desk assistant, newsroom secretary or researcher. The reporter gathers the news in the field and conducts interviews.

Newswriters utilize several sources of information, including news services, material from reporters, and other printed background information to write the copy for news programs. A person might get started writing as a continuity writer responsible for drafting commercials, public service messages and promotional announcements.

The assignment editor is the newsperson in charge of keeping up with current events and giving coverage assignments to the reporters. The assignment editor often functions as assistant to the news director. The news director hires members of the news staff and deals with the station management. Here lies the ultimate responsibility for news coverage and presentation.

On the production side of the news -- that area concerned with actually getting the news on the air -- the entry-level job is often that of production assistant. A production assistant is the person stuck with all the chores no one else has time to do. However, it is an excellent position for learning about every aspect of life in the newsroom.

Production assistants have the opportunity to become field producers, ENG (electronic news gathering) producers, and possibly, depending upon technical know-how, film/tape editors. A Chyron operator is the person who is responsible for all the titles (supers) that appear during the course of a newscast. Other technical people are involved in quality control of the sound and video.

Once you have substantial experience in production, the career ladder points to associate producer, producer, associate director, and director.

To explain in more detail, a field producer coordinates on-site news coverage, working with a reporter, camera operator and any other field personnel. More and more often, a reporter will act as the field producer. In this case, an ENG producer will work with the reporter from the studio, using microwave or satellite connections, to produce the report. An editor, sometimes also the ENG producer, will get involved editing the videotape to a specific length and format. Finally, the technical people, including the Chyron operator, will work with the final copy of the report and prepare it for broadcast.

The associate producer will work with the reporters, editors, ENG producers to ensure the quality and content of the report. In a small station, this position's responsibilities are often handled by the executive producer who works on all the stories that will appear on the nightly newscast.

Directors work in the studio and are the ones who orchestrate the on-air activities. They tell studio camera operators what to do; they give directions about which pre-recorded videotape to run; they work with the floor director who gives instructions to the anchors during the broadcast; they are generally responsible for keeping the newscast running smoothly.

Jobs in news radio are much the same as those in television with the obvious exception of anything visual.

Broadcasting is a heavily unionized industry. Almost every area from technical to writing has a representative group. Besides protecting the rights, wages, and benefits of its workers, unions tend to limit the diversity of job functions within large stations. For example, a writer cannot operate a camera or edit tape even if the station is short on staff for the day.

Working in broadcast journalism can be exciting,

demanding, rewarding, and exhausting. Long hours are typical. Odd hours are not unusual. If you are working on the morning edition of the news you could be working from 5am to 1pm every day, or 6pm to 12 midnight if you are doing the 11 o'clock report. Of course, there are the special events or major breaking news stories that require even longer hours. In many ways, news broadcasting becomes a 24-hour a day job.

Salary

Although the top on-air anchors make 6 figure salaries and sometimes more, they all started at the bottom. Where is the bottom? Entry level salaries of $12,000 are not uncommon and can often be less depending on the location. There is a definite ethic of paying your dues in TV and radio news. However, there are some fortunate people who land TV newswriting jobs or reporting jobs who can earn as much as $25,000 to start. These are rare finds, however.

Job Hunting Tips

Unless you have incredible connections, you will not get a job in broadcast journalism without some directly related experience. There are many good ways to get this experience while a student. In fact, it becomes almost impossible to get experience (in the form of internships) at a local TV and radio commercial stations after you graduate. (Union and government regulations require that all employees of a station be compensated for their work. Students who receive credit for their work can "volunteer" whereas recent grads have no way in.) The only possibility for recent graduates is to work at a cable station or go back to school in a graduate program.

Getting Experience

Almost every commercial radio and television station offers internship programs for the students in the area. This is the best way to get valuable hands-on experience and to observe how a broadcast news program is put together and aired. The contacts you make during an internship may be useful when you are looking for your first job.

An intern's duties might include writing and rewriting copy from news sources, writing public service announcements, editing news service materials, monitoring the news network for possible reports to be used on air, answering phones and taking down stories, and researching and investigating news leads. In fact, news interns often get to do everything the members of the news department do except go on the air, which, as you might guess, is against union rules.

Call or visit the TV and radio stations in the area to get applications. Most will require that you get credit for the internship. Once your application is complete, you should be able to get an internship on one of the many news programs produced in your area. Be prepared to spend a good deal of time (15+ hours) each week on the internship. The more time you spend, the more you will get out of the experience.

Because nearly all internships are unpaid, it may be better to think of your internship as an extracurricular activity and do it during the school year. If you can afford to do an internship during the summer, working full-time, that's great. There are a limited number of paid programs, but these are very highly competitive.

Another way to gain valuable experience for both TV and radio is to work at WHRB, the campus radio station. Here you have the chance to become involved in every aspect, unrestricted by union regulations, of news broadcasting. Admittedly, this experience does not give you exposure to a professional broadcast organization, but combined with an internship experience, it would provide an excellent background.

Naturally, getting some writing experience is important as well. In fact, many present-day TV reporters began as print journalists. Although this route to TV news is not as common today as in the past, it does provide a valuable diversity of experience. Having a collection of published writing samples shows your writing talent and commitment to news and reporting.

Another way to get experience in news broadcasting is through the local cable television stations. As already mentioned, each station must produce a good deal of local programming and they often rely upon interns to produce this material. At a cable station, you may have the unusual opportunity to create, write, edit, produce, and report on-air your own news reports.

To do a good job at a cable station, however, you must take the initiative to come up with the project ideas yourself. Most local access coordinators are hired only to teach people in the community how to use the equipment. The most valuable result of working for a cable station is having tangible results of your work. Having a videotape of four or five reports you have produced becomes a valuable part of your resume packet.

For those who have not had any television experience while in college, cable provides one of the means of getting it. Cable stations cannot compete with commercial stations in production quality and expertise; however, creativity and originality of content can shine through. Having a good resume tape can provide the necessary experience to get an entry-level production or reporting job in commercial television.

A logical question at this point might be: How do I

get all the experience you suggest and still remain a student?! It would be difficult to write for your campus paper, report for the radio station, do three network internships, and create a resume tape at a local cable station. Keep in mind, however, that finding work in broadcast journalism is intensely competitive and that the more experience you have, the better chance you will have of finding a good entry-level position.

Getting the First Job

The first step of any job hunt in broadcast journalism should begin with preparation of the resume packet and resume tape. The resume packet should consist of your resume, any appropriate writing samples, a cover letter, and the resume tape, if necessary.

The resume should be concise, no longer than one page. Make sure your broadcasting experience stands out clearly. Instead of putting the dates of your employment in the far-left column, start with the call letters or organization names for which you worked. A person scanning down the resume who sees WHRB, WGBH, WBZ, and your campus paper will quickly get the idea that you are a serious candidate. Briefly state the highlights of your experience and assume that the reader knows the basic duties of an intern or reporter. Include information that shows your independence, creativity, and resourcefulness; for example, if you travelled to an unusual place, ran the Boston Marathon, or started your own club or organization.

The writing samples should be appropriate samples of your ability to cover a news item thoroughly and concisely. Long feature articles are fine as long as you also include some hard news pieces. If you have sample scripts from radio broadcasts, include them; and, of course, if you have any television writing samples be sure to send them along. Present any writing samples on standard letter-sized paper and make sure that they are easy to read. Include references to the publications and dates of the writing. If you have no samples, it is better to send none than to send an eight-page English paper.

The cover letter should read like a news story on the evening news. Try to avoid the standard form letter approach. Make your reader want to read the rest of the letter by creating a snappy, bold, lead paragraph. Instead of beginning with: "I am a Harvard senior with a degree in English who is dying to enter the field of broadcast journalism," try something like: "Probably the most interesting story I covered in recent years was the controversial resignation of a senior faculty member after charges of sexual harassment." Go on to explain the outcome of your story and your successful experience as a college journalist.

The next paragraphs should briefly outline your goal within broadcast journalism. Be fairly specific. If you want to be in front of the camera, say so. If you'd rather be on the production side, state your reasons and why. Employers are looking for serious, committed entry-level people. There is too much competition for them to work with applicants who "think" they would like work in broadcasting and who "might" be interested in production. As one NBC reporter stated, "We have no time for dilettantes!" This may seem harsh, but the more focused you are, the more any person interviewing you can help.

Close your letter by stating why you would like to work in their organization and that you will contact them in a week to set up a meeting time. Be persistent.

Preparing a resume tape is essential if you want to be an on-air reporter. The videotape should give four or five examples of reports you have given. These reports do not have to have been broadcast. The tape will give your interviewer an idea of your presentation skills, your voice, style, and appearance on screen.

Job hunters prepare their tapes through different means. Sometimes an outstanding intern is given an opportunity to do a few mock reports while out in the field with the regular reporter. Cable stations are an ideal place to prepare a sample tape. Some use their home video equipment to prepare a tape. (Be sure to keep the report simple so that the quality factor is less important.)

If producing a resume tape seems impossible to you, try for a production job and create your tape after you have begun your first job and have easier access to people and equipment. If possible, call upon a career/alumni adviser to critique your tape.

Once you have your resume packet together, you can begin contacting people in the industry. Start with career advisers from your own family/friend connections and from any contacts your career office might have on file. Use the *Broadcasting Yearbook* to compile a list of likely target stations. The *Yearbook* has a list of all the TV stations in the country in order of their market size. *Spot Radio* has a similar listing for radio stations.

The appeal of starting in the largest market stations and at the Networks in New York is great. In New York the key element of your first job is the person for whom you work. If that person takes an interest in your career and is also doing well himself or herself, then chances are you could move up very quickly. However, if this is not the case, you could find yourself stuck without much hope for an upward move. On the other hand, experience with a network will never hurt your resume if you decide to move to a smaller station.

In any case, in New York it will be difficult for you

to gain the variety of experiences possible in a smaller market station. Making a name for yourself in a local TV or radio station should serve you well when trying to break into the Networks. Also, some people prefer local journalism to the Networks.

Another factor to keep in mind when looking for work in the Networks is that hiring has been slow in recent years due to competition from cable and other news sources. Networks are cutting back their staffs, often calling upon freelance production help to fill temporary busy periods. Therefore, getting work at one of the Networks has its risks.

Be sure to use the networking techniques described in the Introduction. The people you meet along the way will be your most important assets as the job hunt progresses.

The guy who hired me had been a salesman 12 years ago at the same company I was working for . . . we were providing programming for KTLA, as a matter of fact. I think there's tremendous value in terms of friends and associates. It's essential because who do people hire? Their friends! A lot of people get hired for jobs not because they're the best person, sad to say, but because they're nice, they represent somebody who can fit into an organization, someone you can have fun with. All of these jobs in the media are high pressure, highly competitive, the stakes are very high. You basically want to work with someone you can go down on the Titanic with comfortably and pleasantly, or visa versa.
- Steve Bell, VP/General Manager - KTLA TV

As you talk with people in broadcasting, you will find that almost every career develops in a different way. Some started as print journalists, some as desk assistants or production assistants, some in radio, some in cable. Some people started their careers in completely different fields, such as teaching, advertising or banking.

Such lack of structure can be frustrating to first-time job hunters. Keep in mind, though, that this type of job hunt encourages creativity, good writing and interviewing skills, and an ability to learn quickly and follow leads. These are just the type of skills you develop as you progress through your liberal arts education.

Case Studies

Frank Mungeam, Producer

*Frank Mungeam graduated in June, 1983, with a Psychology degree. He worked for 3 years as a producer for KING-TV (NBC) in Seattle on the morning talk show **Good Company**. During his fourth year he has been a producer at KATU-TV (ABC) in Portland, OR on their weekly public affairs program **Town Hall**.*

"So, you want to work in broadcasting. What have you done?" This is the most frightening question a recent graduate can face. But the question is inevitable. So you better have an answer!

By my junior year at Harvard I was certain I wanted to go into broadcasting. For the next two years, I worked to `package' myself to be ready to answer the `experience' question.

I joined WHRB as a freshman. By graduation, I'd done everything from a late night, new-wave rock show to broadcasting Harvard football. WHRB offered a unique opportunity for hands-on broadcast experience. In my junior year, I became station manager. From that position, I gained valuable experience managing people -- and a resume item that landed me my first job! But more on that later.

I spent the summer before my senior year as an

intern in the Governor's press office at the State House in Boston. The position helped me sharpen my writing skills, get an inside peek at media coverage of a political figure, and gave me my first portfolio entry -- published articles!

All this experience looked good to me. But I still had no TV knowledge. How would I convince a TV station I knew anything about television? So, in my senior year, I began scrambling to find a TV internship. I was too late to get into WBZ's program, and WGBH needed a full-time person. Also, both required interns to receive academic credit. I was sure that was impossible at Harvard. Then, at the Office of Career Services, I found out about "independent study." So I looked up the local cable TV stations and started calling. I discovered that some stations didn't offer internships, some were totally disorganized, and one -- thankfully -- was interested! I found a History professor who agreed to act as my `independent (invisible) advisor' and began riding the subway and bus, twice a week, to Revere . . . and KBLE TV.

At KBLE, I truly `played at TV.' I was the anchor of a 5-minute, nightly NEWS UPDATE, shot video in the field, learned elementary editing and directing, and produced stories. Without the independent study course credit, I never could have spared the time.

The cable experience completed my `package.' By getting radio, writing, and broadcast experience during college, I was trying to demonstrate a serious commitment to a career in broadcasting. At least, that was the intention!

Looking for work was the hardest part for me. I compiled a list of TV stations from a book at Career Services. I wrote my cover letter and braced myself for a mass mailer -- one hundred shots in the dark. I also kept and eye on the OCS Newsletter. There, I found a tiny listing for a paid summer internship at a TV station in Seattle, Washington. It caught my eye because the program consisted of several weeks in each of the different TV departments. It sounded like a great chance to scout the territory. I applied with a cover letter and resume and had a phone interview with the station manager. As we spoke, I noticed his interest in my WHRB experience. Would you believe he started out as station manager at Dartmouth's radio station! The morning of my graduation from Harvard, I received a phone call offering me the position in Seattle.

In the four years that followed, I've worked with more than a dozen interns. A few were terrible. Most were good. Several were great. I know of only two who've 'made it' since in TV. Some very good are still waiting. This fact has reinforced the feeling I had as I landed in Seattle that first day: in such a competitive field, you're lucky to get one chance -- you'd better use it! In that spirit, I worked harder during my ten weeks in Seattle than at any time before or since (including exam period!). At the end of the internship, I was offered positions in news, sales and programming!

I learned some useful lessons during my internship. In hindsight, I would try to arrange to have a TV internship before going to a cable station. The advantage of cable is unrestricted hands-on access. But I didn't know what to do with the equipment, and the opportunity was somewhat wasted. Typically, people in cable will not have the expertise to teach you. That's why a TV internship is a better first step. Though union (and slavery!) laws restrict hands-on access, you are surrounded by knowledgeable professionals eager to impart wisdom.

My TV internship also showed me the reality of day-to-day life in TV. I flew to Seattle with TV-Reporter aspirations. After all, that's what viewers of TV see -- the on-camera people. I soon realized that the degree of specialization in TV news limits the influence of the reporter. A photographer shoots his story, an editor cuts it, and the producer decides where it will run, how long it goes, and what angle is taken. The other negative, for me, was the reactive nature of the job: you hurry up and wait for something to happen!

Along with this alienation came a new discovery: "producing!" In local TV, a programming department is responsible for the station's non-news shows -- daily talk and magazine programs, weekly issue-oriented public affairs shows, and specials. On these shows, the producer determines show topics, selects the guests and pre-interviews them, then prepares the host for the interview with notes and suggested questions. The host's concerns, by contrast can seem superficial at times. Attention to appearance, time cues, and addressing the correct camera often cancel out the pleasures of being the on-camera interviewer and being recognized around town. What I consider the 'content decisions' have already been made -- by producers -- before the host becomes involved. I chose to become a producer because the content decisions were the ones that mattered most to me.

Larry Kahn, Radio Station Operations Manager

Larry began his radio career at WHRB as a sports announcer. His academic concentration was in economics. He is now Operations Manager at WCOD-FM in Hyannis, Massachusetts.

THE GAME - 1986. End Zone, Section 20. Sitting with most of the Currier House Class of 1983, most of whom haven't seen or heard from me in one to three years. But they all seem to have formed the same memory of what their classmate "The Voice of Harvard Sports", who went into radio, is doing now . . .

"Hey Larry! Almost didn't recognize you! How's it feel not to be in the press box? Still in radio on the Cape? Aren't you a D.J. or something??"

-- Well, not exactly. I'm the Operations Manager at WCOD in Hyannis. Been there since graduation.

"So . . . you on the air at all?" (Management titles in radio don't seem to hold their interest.)

-- Umm, yeah. I sometimes fill in on sports for our morning show. (laughing) They call me Sid Michaels!

"Sid Michaels!!"

-- It's a long story . . . .

I came to Harvard with every intention of fulfilling those three basic goals of higher education -- good grades, good times, and getting a job with good money. As a financial aid student from a middle-class family which placed a high value on education as a means, if not necessarily an end (my father is a semi-frustrated 30-year veteran of the public school rat race), I majored in Economics for all the right reasons. It let me take related courses in everything from Folklore and Mythology to Evolutionary Biology, it was great preparation for business school, and a business degree from Harvard was an automatic financial payoff on a resume.

That's the philosophy I stayed with right through first term of my senior year. Along the way, I fleshed out my college experience with work-study employment, house intramurals and committee work, and primarily with a heavy commitment to WHRB. At many times, Harvard Radio became a first priority, rather than an extracurricular activity.

I competed for a postition in sports and studio engineering. Luck, and some verbal ability when it came to athletics (as opposed to physical talents, of which I have few), got me on the air announcing Harvard basketball and football games by sophomore year. A discovery that I actually did have creativity -- not in music or art, but in speaking, writing, and commercial production in the studio -- fed my other needs . . . like ego, comic relief, study breaks.

Taking over as Sports Director my junior year, I then was able to actually apply some education, like marketing, to my daily radio pursuits. I negotiated advertising contracts, traded out rental cars, promoted "Harvard Sports" to the Greater Boston listening area and to the major Boston press, wrote commercial copy, managed press passes for our reporters to Bruins and Celtics games, and basically had a fantastic learning experience. In short, I was bitten by the radio bug.

Not that I wasn't enjoying just about everything about Harvard, and about getting a Harvard education. But somewhere along the line I developed a bad case of morality. I didn't have enough time, like many of my friends, to work with Phillips Brooks House or at some other community service endeavor (maybe I didn't make time, but I don't think so). Yet, the more I read, heard, and otherwise absorbed about the business world, the less and less appealing it sounded. I don't like ties. I'm not crazy about corporate politics. I didn't like the picture painted of "unions" and "government." Radio, at least from my vantage point, combined all the good parts of business with the humaneness I was comfortable with.

The summer of '82 helped confirm those attitudes. I interned in the newsroom at WHDH-Boston. I didn't like being a "hard-news" reporter. I did love the people whom I saw day-to-day work crazy hours at a crazy jobs for a terrific reason. The better they made the radio station, the more popular it became. The more listeners they obtained, the more advertisers they could sell commercial time to. The more commercial time they sold, the more profitable they became, and the more money they had to spend on providing great news, great music, and great public service to the community. Sound ideal? I thought so.

That thought stayed with me through the spring of my senior year, when I decided to try and get a full-time job in radio. I figured I had nothing to lose and everything to gain (although I did take the GMAT's in January of that year, just to be safe). I spent spring break making up audition tapes of my work as an announcer and commercial producer and sent them with my resume to every station in the New England area I thought big enough to afford someone in either sports or advertising. Basically, I was pitching for any entry-level position. Ten days after 40 of those fantastic packages of my talents went into the mail, I had received zero answers. Day 11 was my time to start follow-up phone calls. The Sales Manager at WCOD-Hyannis beat me to it. I was lucky.

Two trips to the Cape and two nervous interviews

later, I had accepted a position as a Sales Assistant (later termed "marketing coordinator") for $225 a week. I was told there would be plenty of room for growth and that it was a tremendous learning opportunity. Was I naive? Sure, just as naive as when I brilliantly assessed what a wonderful business philosophy radio stations have (see above)!!

It is now December of 1986. As my classmates were reminded via my business card, I am now a middle manager at WCOD. I handle promotion of the station, and contests on the station. I work with community groups and charities on public service campaigns. I do market research and help write marketing material for our Sales staff to sell with to advertisers. I handle logistical details from overseeing our computer-generated program logs, commercial scheduling and music playlist, to remote broadcasts from all over Cape Cod. I work with our Program Director in managing our Air Staff, and with our Sales Manager on supporting our Sales staff, Traffic Manager, and Copywriter (which I was before being promoted to Operations Manager.)

I've successfully coordinated, promoted, and directed the Cape Cod Chowder Festival, Johnny Kelley Road Race, and Christmas lighting of the Village Green. I've been in fantasy parades, at bridge parties, and on top of 250-foot monuments in 60-mph winds holding an antenna. I've also coached the softball team, filled the Coke machine, unclogged the toilet, and stood in the rain and cold at more store "grand openings featuring a live broadcast by WCOD" than I care to remember.

I don't wear a tie (well, rarely). I laugh a lot. I get great satisfaction out of letters from individuals and community organizations that have been helped by a WCOD promotion or public service effort of some kind. I deal with the daily frustrations of managing people who aren't products of the Ivy League (but that's not the reason I get frustrated by them), and very rarely do either of the two things I enjoyed most at WHRB -- broadcast sporting events or produce commercials (yes, I occasionally fill in on the morning show as "Sports Reporter Sid Michaels." It's the station's way of humoring me.) I just recently could afford to get my own apartment and a new car and still don't make much more than $20,000 a year.

But so far I'm happy. Not everyone I met at THE GAME '86 was. Some of them wished they'd taken a route similar to mine. I didn't encourage them. If you really are thinking of radio as a career, not "media" or "communications," give me a call anytime at WCOD. I may talk you out of your plans . . . but if you've been bitten by the same bug as I, you'll pick up advice you can't find in any textbook.

Bibliography

Books

Career Opportunities in Television and Video, Maxine and Robert Reed, Facts On File Publications, New York, 1982.
A useful listing of job titles with career paths for each job title. Gives job description, salary, educational or experience necessary, and a career ladder telling what the next career step may be.

Creative Careers, Gary Blake and Robert Bly, Wiley Press, New York, 1983.
Excellent chapters on television and film. Very good bibliographies.

Dream Jobs, Gary Blake and Robert Bly, Wiley Press, New York, 1985.
An insightful description of various career fields,

including a chapter on cable television. Has a very good bibliography for each chapter.

Inside Track, Ross and Kathryn Petras, Vintage Books, New York, 1986.
Focuses on individual companies, some in television, including CNN, CBS, and ABC.

Opportunities in Cable Television, Jan Bone, VGM Career Horizons, Chicago, 1984.
Basic, informative guide to the cable television industry. Focuses on job opportunities and job hunting techniques in this part of the film/TV industry.

Women in Communications, Alice Fins, VGM Career Horizons, Skokie, Illinois, 1979.
Case studies of the careers of women in broadcasting and other communications careers.

Directories

1989 Internships, F&W Publications, Cincinnati, Ohio, annual.
Describes internships and summer jobs in television, along with other categories. Eligibility and application information for each listing.

Broadcasting's Yearbook, Broadcasting Publications, Washington, D.C., annual.
Valuable information about television and radio industries, including market statistics, station addresses, phone numbers and other pertinent details about broadcasting. Compliments the TV Factbooks.

Getting Work Experience, Betsy Bauer, Dell Publishing, New York, New York, 1985.
Among other listings, describes summer internship

programs in broadcast journalism. Gives pertinent application information including pay scales (if any), qualifications desired, and deadlines.

International Television Almanac, Quigley Publishing Company, New York, annual.
Contains a who's who of prominent individuals in the television community, lists of television companies, and producers, as well as other information and listings about industry-related suppliers.

New England Media Directory, Burrelle's Media Directories, Livingston, New Jersey, annual.
Listing of all media sources in the New England area, including addresses, phone numbers, and key personnel of television stations.

New York Media Directory, Burrelle's Media Directories, Livingston, New Jersey, annual.
Listing of all media sources in New York, including addresses, phone numbers, and key personnel of television stations.

Spot Radio, Standard Rates & Data Corp., Washington, D.C., monthly.
List all major radio stations in the country, including size, format, and key personnel of each.

The Student Guide to Mass Media Internships, Vol 2, Ronald Claxton, Intern Research Group, University of Colorado, Boulder, Colorado, annual.
List internships available in television, pay scales and deadlines.

World Radio TV Handbook, Billboard Limited, New York, New York, annual.
Main section of the book contains detailed informa-

tion, country by country, on the radio and television stations of every country in the world.

Periodicals

Broadcasting, Broadcasting Inc., New York, New York, weekly.
Information on television and radio broadcasting. Focuses primarily on the business side; however, does have occasional job listings.

The Ross Reports, Television Index Inc., New York, New York, monthly.
Primarily a resource for actors; lists all prime-time, daytime, and news programs with information about production location, producers' names, and format. Also has four page "blue" section with late-breaking news about new shows and TV movies.

Chapter 5

Book Publishing

Book publishers may be overheard referring to their work, loftily, as a profession; realistically, as a business; ruefully, as a gamble. It is essentially a business -- probably more fun than most. It is something of a gamble, too, for it involves considerable risks, even when its effort is directed towards educational or specialized audiences that can pretty well be estimated in advance. But it is a business that has strong professional overtones; it serves all the professions and it has room for a remarkable number of professional skills and non-publishing professional backgrounds.
-Chandler B. Grannis, from
What Happens in Book Publishing

After spending some time and money each semester buying books for your coursework, you might have the impression that the book industry is flourishing. It is not uncommon to spend $25 on one text! In fact, however, the book publishing industry has not been growing a great deal for the past several years. Between 1983 and 1984, for example, net book sales rose only 0.5%. On the other hand, this does not mean that book publishing is in peril of extinction: in 1984 there were 16,000 book publishers in the United States, compared to 12,000 in 1981.

So, what is the climate of the industry? Book publishers face a very challenging future. The general public is demanding a greater variety of books on many different subjects and in many different media. Instructional videocassettes, computer software, and other multi-media presentations are being demanded. The increase in the number of publishers in the past five years indicates a reaction to the demand for greater variety. Many publishers are specializing in certain subject areas or focusing on special reader groups.

Industry Profile

As you stroll through Harvard Square, browsing in its many bookstores, you are experiencing the efforts of professionals involved in only one side of the publishing business: trade publishing. "Trade" refers to those books sold through retailers to the general public: works of general fiction and nonfiction, biography, poetry and literary works. The book publishing industry also includes textbook, religious, children's, scholarly, technical, scientific, medical and professional publishing, book clubs, and most recently, electronic publishing. A few of the most popular areas of publishing are described in more detail below.

Trade Book Publishing

The fact that the "trade" element of publishing only accounts for about 30% of the industry's total sales is surprising to most people new to the book business. However, trade publishing is the most glamorous and visual element of the industry. The "best sellers" and best-selling authors who appear on the Today Show are all involved in trade publishing. But the sobering fact is that the average hardcover book sells only about 5000 copies. Consequently, publishers often release their books first as paperbacks instead of as hardcovers. The savings in production costs allow more books to be published. You may have noticed how the price of a quality trade paperback has gone up in recent years.

Trade publishers often rely on "blockbusters" to make the difference between a successful year and a year in the red. A blockbuster is a best-selling novel that not only sells well, but is adapted for motion picture release and republished in different languages overseas. Large fees, often in the millions of dollars, are charged for "movie rights" and overseas distribution. Profits soar

even further when a book or series of books tie in with the
sale of non-book items such as toys, posters, and cloth-
ing.

Educational/Textbook Publishing

Many of the largest publishers in this country rely
upon their educational publishing divisions to keep the
company earning healthy profits. Educational/textbook
publishing earns about 42% of the industry's sales every
year.

The reason behind this fact becomes clear when you
start to think about the tremendous volume of publishing required to keep the average school system afloat.
Textbooks, workbooks, filmstrips, teacher's guides,
supplementary materials, computer software all fall into
the category of educational publishing. Every school
system in the country expects publishers to provide up-
to-date materials at the end of each school year when
teachers start to plan the next academic program.

The crucial sales question for educational publishers is whether or not a book will be adopted for use by a
school system, or even more significantly, an entire state.
Some states -- California and Texas, for example -- have
statewide committees that review and select textbooks
for use in the state school systems. The committee
usually decides on four or five texts from which teachers
can choose. Therefore, a publisher will lose all sales
opportunities within an entire state if it is not selected by
the adoption committee. Losing an adoption can mean
a loss of literally millions of dollars in potential sales.

Scholarly Book Publishing

Scholarly book publishers are often university presses or small specialized publishers. Many people are

interested in the "ivory tower" of book publishing because they are under the impression that only works of the highest quality and merit are published. University presses are often subsidized by the sponsoring university and the "ivory tower" concept was fairly accurate until the recession years hit hard in the 70's.

Today, however, many scholarly publishers must keep an eye on the marketability of their lists of books. If they cannot make a profit, or at least break even, support and funding may begin to evaporate. University presses are expanding their lists to include books of greater and more general appeal. Although it is rare to see a scholarly press's book on the best seller list, one is often surprised by the variety of titles that sometimes appear

The large university presses are organized along the same lines as a trade house, with the frequent addition of an editorial advisory board comprised of faculty members who review manuscripts in their particular fields. In smaller university presses, staff members may have to perform several different functions such as writing ad copy, proofreading, or helping with production.

Career Profiles

Book publishing is like any other business in that it has its accountants, lawyers, bookkeepers, and managers. Those careers special to the book publishing world will be discussed here. They fall into three areas: editorial, production & design, advertising & sales.

Editorial

The world of the book editor has been romanticized as one of three-martini lunches at four-star restaurants. As with most myths, this one contains only small elements of truth. While expensive lunches do take place, the editor's job is primarily one spent reading, editing, and corresponding.

A career as a trade book editor usually begins as an editorial assistant. An editorial assistant's job is to organize: files, manuscripts, editors' schedules, authors' visits, department meetings, etc. There is a fair bit of typing involved as well: typing letters to authors, rejection letters accompanying unwanted manuscripts, memos to other departments, editorial reports. Also, the editorial assistant will be called upon to do proofreading and copy editing. After a few months of this kind of "apprenticeship," you will certainly know how the editorial offices at a publishing house work.

However, beyond the clerical aspect of the job, there is often the opportunity to do a great deal of reading. The editorial assistant is often the first filter through which all unsolicited manuscripts from aspiring authors must pass. It is the job of the editorial assistant to read and report on all such submissions. Only the best from the "slush" pile make it past the assistant's desk. Sometimes an editorial assistant will "discover" a hot new author. If you love books, reading them, and following the lives of those who write them, you should make it through your apprenticeship as an editorial assistant.

After one to two years, an editorial assistant looks for a way to become an assistant or associate editor. This job brings more responsibility, sometimes less clerical work, and an increase in salary. Assistant or associate editors are sometimes responsible for working with authors, suggesting rewrites, additions, and cuts to the manuscript. The associate editor also works with the other departments, following the prepared manuscripts through all phases of production and marketing.

As you move higher in the editorial ranks to editor,

managing editor, executive editor, and editor-in-chief, you will become more and more involved with the business side of publishing. You will negotiate contracts with authors, help plan marketing strategies, dream up ideas for new books, solicit manuscripts from "name" authors, and generally become involved in helping decide the overall editorial and managerial policies of the publishing house.

It should be mentioned that editorial jobs in other segments of publishing, especially textbook publishing, vary with the type of book being published. A textbook editor's job, for example, involves becoming familiar with the curricula in whatever subject area he or she is working: science, math, sociology, elementary school subjects, etc. Often, a textbook editor will have spent some time teaching. The goal is to produce a high-quality product that will win statewide adoption in several states.

Those interested in college textbook editing will often be required to spend some time visiting college professors as sales representatives. This sales preparation is often seen as a necessary part of learning to be an effective editor. The thinking is that if the editor is sensitive to professors' needs, there is a better chance that the text will be a success.

Within the area of editing is the role of the literary agent. A literary agent represents authors to publishers and acts as a negotiator and advocate for the author. Recently, the agent has gained a good deal of influence in the publishing community because publishers have less time and staff to devote to reading unsolicited manuscripts. Therefore, publishers have come to rely on agents to provide them with new ideas and new talent.

Working as an assistant for an agent involves many

of the same tasks as an editorial assistant. Most agencies are very small (5 to 10 people), so the assistant is called upon to carry out a variety of jobs, including reading manuscripts, writing reports, keeping authors up-to-date on the progress of their manuscripts, typing correspondence and filing, and arranging meetings with authors, agents and publishers.

Assistants may sometimes move up within the agency to become full-fledged agents if an opening occurs. However, more often, assistants may move up by going to a publishing house as an assistant or associate editor or becoming agents at other firms.

Production & Design

If the job of editor does not appeal, but you are still intrigued by the world of books, the areas of design and production offer interesting possibilities. People in the design and production departments are responsible for designing and manufacturing the finished product.

For those in the design department, the job primarily revolves around the task of creating a product that is easy to read and, at the same time, attractive and noticeable. Most people in the design department have some kind of design school background. They begin as assistant designers and are expected to act, as do editors, as apprentices for a number of years. The designer's apprenticeship usually involves doing all the preparation work for the senior designer. Also, there may be a fair bit of paste-up and simple layout work to do. At some point, when the novice designer shows the skill to do so, he or she is given the responsibility for an entire project, much as the associate editor or editor is assigned an author and manuscript.

Those in the production department are responsible

for taking the designers' specifications and actually making the book: working with the typesetters, editors, and designers during the proof stages, ordering paper, scheduling the printing and binding, and, most importantly, keeping everything moving along on schedule.

The production assistant is the entry-level person in the department. He or she usually works as the production supervisor's assistant, including scheduling meetings, checking the progress of all the books currently in production, typing correspondence to suppliers (paper merchants, printers, binders, etc.), estimating lengths of books. A production assistant will soon learn all the steps necessary to producing a book on time and under budget.

After a year or so, a production assistant will most likely be promoted to become a specialist in one production area for a while: ordering all the paper needed for upcoming books, arranging for the binding of the books once they are printed, or working with the typesetters. If especially good at organizational tasks, the production specialist may be asked to do the scheduling of new books.

The production director (usually coming from the ranks of production specialists) is the person responsible for seeing that all the production stages fit together perfectly so that books will be produced in the shortest time and in the most cost-effective way possible. After all, a publisher cannot start to make money until the books are produced.

Advertising and Sales

The advertising and sales division is responsible for the final aspect of the book selling process: getting the book into the bookstore (sales) and making readers aware of its existence (advertising). The job of selling books is that of the sales representative or book traveller (the title for the position may change, depending on the publishing house). The task of selling a book is unlike almost any other sales job. In one sense, you are selling an idea. No one has time to read every book before deciding to buy, so the salesperson must be able to convince the book buyers that this is just the book they would like to read without having read it. Therefore, the sales rep must know the bookstore buyers well enough to know the types of books that sell well in that particular bookstore.

The sales rep usually has a defined geographic territory and visits every bookstore in his or her area. There are no well-defined entry-level positions. Everyone begins as a sales rep. The career ladder for a sales rep usually leads to larger, more important territories or to a management position in the home office. Management positions often lead to those higher in the publishing house and often involve determining sales and marketing strategies and responsibility for all the selling activity in the house. Many sales reps branch out on their own to represent more than one publisher and become independents.

The word "sales" often scares off most who initially see themselves as book people. Consider, though, the type of selling you would be doing. In the case of trade book publishing, the sales rep's job is more one of a consultant and inventory manager than one of the hardcore salesperson.

After all, if you are working for a reputable and respected publisher, every bookstore owner will want to buy your books. The primary question is which books from your list should they buy and how many of each? Here, the sales rep becomes a consultant, recommending a purchase strategy based on past sales of similar books in that bookstore. If you do your job well, you will probably make some very good friends along the way. Besides, most bookstore owners are very interesting people . . . Why else would they be selling such a risky item as a book if they weren't committed to a life surrounded by books?!

Those involved in the advertising of new books often find that they must take on many different kinds of roles. Not only do they have to create and place advertising in different media, but they must get exposure for the author, plan publicity, and work with the literary press. The advertising function at a publishing house often takes on many different names: promotion, marketing, and publicity. If the publisher is large enough, there may be several departments, all involved in one kind of marketing effort or another.

A career in advertising begins, as do most of the careers in publishing, as an assistant, getting training on the job. Many advertising, promotion, and marketing assistants begin with research tasks involving market and media studies. Compiling lists of potential promotional media is an invaluable resource for most publishers. Because of the prohibitive cost of national advertising, most of the promotional activity is centered on getting free publicity: reviews in national papers and magazines, author interviews on television and radio, author appearances at bookstores, etc. Arranging for such publicity takes a good deal of phone work and mailings. It is not uncommon for a publisher to send review copies of a new book to all the major newspapers and magazines in the country, a task which sometimes requires hundreds of books.

Careers in advertising/promotion lead to senior positions which may involve planning the strategy for the release of new titles, sometimes including motion picture releases, merchandising campaigns, and other innovative techniques to sell books.

Salary

Book publishers are notorious for paying their entry-level employees poorly. Editorial assistants may be offered as little as $11,000 to start. More typical is a salary in the low teens. Those in sales can earn salaries above $20,000 with commission, but the base salary remains in the mid-teens. Furthermore, this compensation schedule is even more so discouraging because most publishers are located in Manhattan, the high-rent capital of the U.S. Therefore, what would be a low salary anyway, becomes impossible in New York. The publishing industry will have to wake up to the fact that the backbone of its young talent will be lost unless it starts paying them realistic wages. The industry cannot survive by hiring only those who can afford to take the jobs.

Take heart though, because, as your career progresses, so does your salary. You can never expect to earn megabucks in publishing unless you become a superstar salesperson, editor or publisher, however.

Job-Hunting Tips

As with most of the other media, publishing is a highly competitive field. Preparation is the key to gaining employment in the top publishing houses. There are several types of research you can do on the industry. The first is reading some basic texts on the fundamentals of book publishing. See the bibliography at the end of this chapter.

Also, you should begin reading *Publisher's Weekly*

magazine. Every publisher and bookstore owner reads this magazine. It outlines all the current news in the industry. It also lists a limited number of job openings in the back section. The most valuable information, oddly enough, comes from the advertising. Since most of the major publishers advertise in *Publishers Weekly*, you can get a good idea of the works all these publishers are producing. This information should come in handy when you are putting together your target list and writing cover letters.

Visit bookstores, but don't just browse. Make this enjoyable project educational as well. Note which books you see first, the various prices and price ranges, the sections, the other customers and shopping patterns. You should begin to make some interesting observations about different marketing techniques and problems in the book industry, information that will be valuable to you as an editor or sales representative, and definitely as a job hunter.

Become familiar with the industry directory, The *Literary Market Place (LMP)*. The *LMP* has all sorts of interesting information about every major publisher in the country, including names, addresses, phone numbers, key executives, the number of titles they publish each year, and what sorts of books they publish. Also, the *LMP* contains information about services and businesses related to publishing, such as literary agents, freelance editors, copyeditors and proofreaders, book distributors, manufacturers and wholesalers, and professional groups and associations. Other information that can be found in the *LMP* includes the results of all the major book awards for the year.

Of course, talking with people who are involved in the book industry provides invaluable information. Don't forget about your alumni contacts, academic advisers, and professors. Many of them have been involved in the publishing process as consultants, editors, and authors.

Getting Experience

If you can gain any firsthand exposure to the book publishing industry before you graduate, that will put you one step ahead of the competition for entry-level jobs. There are several good ways to get this type of experience. First, many publishers are happy to take on interns. If you can find 10 to 15 hours a week to spend helping a local publishing firm, you will quickly learn a great deal about the day-to-day demands of the book publishing world. Use *The Student Guide to Mass Media Internships, Getting Work Experience,* and *1989 Internships* to identify selected programs. Use *Publishers Weekly* and the *LMP* to add to your list.

Part-time work in a bookstore is excellent book publishing experience. Although checking inventory and shelving books may seem like mundane work, you will discover which kinds of books sell, who publishes the most successful books, how books are ordered, what the busy seasons are, and which marketing tactics work and don't work.

Naturally, work on a student magazine or similar publication will be valuable. Any demonstration of some editing, proofreading, and/or copyediting will be a plus on your resume.

For those of you who can't find the time to do internships or part-time jobs, there are a number of postgraduate summer programs that offer formal training and introduction to the book business. The Radcliffe Publishing Procedures Course is one course that, within an 8-week summer session, introduces you to the world of publishing with professionals from New York publishing as teachers and lecturers. There are similar programs at the University of Denver, Stanford, N.Y.U. and many other programs across the country. Consult the *Guide to Book Publishing Courses* for a complete list of summer and other programs in publishing.

Getting the First Job

Occasionally, entry-level opportunities in publishing will be listed in *Publishers Weekly*. However, for the most part, you must rely on your own legwork to uncover entry-level jobs. Use the techniques of networking described in the Introduction to uncover job leads.

Spend some time writing a good cover letter, one that shows your writing style and editing prowess (make sure there are no typos). Your resume should highlight any publishing experience you have had, including extracurricular activities. Often it is a good idea to have a separate section entitled Publishing/Writing Experience. In this way, you can focus your resume and include paid and unpaid experience in the same section.

Finding work in the book publishing world depends primarily on your requirements for that first job. Where would you like to live? How much money do you need to make? Although there are book publishers throughout the country, New York City is the center of publishing in this country. There are a few other cities across the country with a good deal of publishing activity, but none even comes close to the number of publishers in New York. Therefore, if you would like to work outside Manhattan, realize that you are limiting your possibilities.

Keep in mind that most people in the publishing world love books. If you can convey to these people your appreciation for and understanding of the publishing world, you should have good success in your job hunt.

Case Study

Adrienne Weiss, Marketing Assistant

Adrienne had a continuing interest in books and publishing throughout her undergraduate years. Her studies focused on the history and literature of France. She had a summer internship at a publishing house and worked in a library on campus. She is a marketing assistant at Harvard University Press.

For various reasons that remain obscure to me, I decided after I graduated from college to get into book publishing. I had enjoyed the internship I had done at the Atlantic Monthly Press the summer after my sophomore year. Also, I liked the job I had in a library as an undergraduate, so publishing seemed like a reasonable idea. (I had not been particularly career-oriented in college.) Although I knew that the center of the publishing universe was New York, I decided to see if I could find a job in Boston.

Once I'd decided to look into publishing, I started reading everything I could find on the subject, including *Publishers Weekly*, publishers' catalogs and books on the trade. Finding out about the industry helped me understand how the industry worked and better defined for me what the options were. The reading I did turned out to be incredibly useful as I started talking to people; it helped me ask more sophisticated questions, which led to more interesting and valuable conversations with career advisers. And even a little book learning sets one apart from all the other eager publishing hopefuls (and there are a lot, but most of them don't bother to do their homework).

For a long time my research was entirely a solitary experience. I got as far as looking up career advisors at the Office of Career Services, but couldn't force myself to contact them. ("I'll just wait until I've done a little more reading . . . ," I would say to myself.) This was a big mistake. No amount of book learning can replace talking with people. Informational interviews are invaluable. However, it helps to go into an interview having done your homework: people are usually happy to talk about what they do, but they don't want to lecture on the structure of the publishing industry. It also helps to know something about the career adviser's company. Look at its announcement catalogs for the past few seasons and get an idea of what sort of books it does and who its big authors are. Go to bookstores and look at the company's books to get a feel for its design philosophy. Check out the *New York Times* bestseller list for the publisher's books. And then use all this information to have a more productive and informative interview and to show that you are thinking like a publisher. (The more people you talk to, the more you will get a sense of what sort of things publishers find important.)

I benefited greatly from the information interviews I had in Boston. It was good to get into actual publishing houses and to see what the people and environment were like. (Try to have interviews in people's offices, not over lunch, because it gives you a better idea of what goes on at their companies.) I asked everyone I talked to if they knew of anyone else who might be willing to speak to me, and so each interview engendered more contacts. (Never leave an interview without asking for names, especially if you think the interview went well. Most people will come up with a few names at least. And these people will feel an obligation to speak to you because you've been referred by their friend.)

I found the job listings in the *Boston Globe, Publishers Weekly*, at OCS, and at the Women's Educational and Industrial Union pretty unsatisfactory. Most entry-level positions never show up in those places and when they do, the positions are often filled by the time you see the listing. I wouldn't suggest ignoring them, but you shouldn't rely on them exclusively. My best leads were from my increasingly growing network. I followed up every interview with a thank-you letter, and then wrote periodically to the people who had been particularly helpful to tell them I was still looking, in case they heard of anything. You have to be in the right place at the right time, so I figured I'd better be in as many places at as many times as I could manage. My letters were always polite and upbeat and I don't think I annoyed too many people.

After a month of information interviewing, I answered a *PW* ad for a part-time paste-up assistant for a freelance designer. I got no response from my letter or the three or four phone messages I had left. As it turned out, the designer had hired someone before he even got my letter, but by the time I called for the fourth time -- and actually got through to the man -- the person he'd hired had already quit, and so he was looking again. He hired me with no experience for $5 per hour to do paste-up a few times a week. This gave me experience working with mechanicals and time to think about design considerations.

After a month with the designer, I replied to an ad in the *Globe* for a proofreading position at Cahners Publishing Company. I got a reply saying that the position I'd applied for had been filled, but that I should consider another position they had open: production assistant in the newsletter division. Although I had no interest in the kind of publishing Cahners did (trade journals for industry), I took the job because I was eager to work full-time and the position offered more responsibility. I had no idea how wide the gap was between this sector of the publishing profession and the trade book sector. The editorial philosophy and marketing approach was different and the people who worked at Cahners seemed isolated from the Boston book publishing community, so I really wasn't involved with the publishing in which I was interested. The job really didn't suit me, although I got some good experience from it: line editing, proofreading, paste-up (I took a course in layout while at Cahners), word processing, working with printers and typesetters. After six months, I was looking for a job again.

This time, I was much more aggressive about contacting people and following up letters with phone calls. I talked to several career advisers, and one of them arranged a paid internship for me in the production department of Houghton Mifflin's trade division. Even though I was only typing data into a computer, the job got me into a trade house where I could look around and see what it had to offer. This experience introduced me to a lot of people who have subsequently been very helpful. I worked at Houghton Mifflin for two months, at which point I got a job as an editorial assistant in the College Division at Little, Brown & Co.

I found out about the position at Little Brown in a funny, roundabout way, which illustrates why you should never ignore a contact, no matter how remote. During my senior year in college, an acquaintance of mine had given me the name of her boarding school roommate, who was working at Little Brown and might be willing to talk to me about publishing. When I finally called her (eight months later!), it was her last day at Little Brown and her boss hadn't replaced her yet. I went in to speak to her boss, but she had pretty much chosen someone already. She passed my name along to the English Textbook Editor, whose assistant had just given notice. I interviewed with the English Editor and was offered the job.

Little Brown was a good experience and I stayed there for 15 months. I worked for an excellent editor who was genuinely interested in furthering my career and whose list [list of titles for which she was responsible] was one of Little Brown's more important ones (which gave her a bigger budget and more clout than other editors). Also, there was always extra work to be done and I got to do some interesting projects on overtime and on a freelance basis. I learned a lot more from my freelance projects than from my duties as an editorial assistant. (Freelancing is an terrific way to gain experience, make contacts, develop new skills, and improve your resume. It demands diligence and hustling to get work.) I enjoyed working with the Little Brown authors and their manuscripts, but slowly came to realize that I didn't want to stay in textbook publishing. I didn't like the emphasis placed on creating a product to fit a market need and on imitating the successful texts of other publishers. I decided that I wanted to go into high-brow trade publishing -- quality fiction and the kind of nonfiction that borders on the academic. Again, I started reading -- this time about advertising, direct mail and publicity -- and when I had learned enough of the basics to sound reasonably intelligent, I began informational interviewing with marketing types. Almost right away a friend of mine from Bookbuilders (a Boston publishing group) told me about a direct mail position at Harvard University Press. Harvard is an academic press that does a lot of trade books, so its list was right up my alley.

My experience at Harvard in direct mail promotion has taught me about the various components of the promotion effort for each book and about the different audiences. It has also given me experience writing copy, working with designers, typesetters (including telecommunications copy), and printers, and using computer spreadsheet programs to track profit and loss.

In addition to work experience, I have been active in

several publishing organizations: Bookbuilders of Boston, Boston Publishing Group, Women's National Book Association, and Women in Scholarly Publishing. Being active in these groups has been helpful because it provides opportunities to meet people from other publishing houses in casual situations. But Bookbuilders has been especially valuable for me because I have been involved in committee work. Volunteer organizations always need more helpers and working on a committee is a great way to meet people and show what you can do. I have worked in more responsible positions on more interesting projects for Bookbuilders than in any of my actual jobs. And, I have used Bookbuilders contacts over and over again for job references and advice.

So that is what I've done in the past three years. Because of the number of lateral moves I've made across departments (production-editorial-marketing), I have not developed enough strength in any one area to move up. On the other hand, I have a broad experience which helps me understand the larger picture of publishing better.

Publishing careers tend to involve infuriatingly long apprenticeships. What's worse, publishing attracts bright, energetic, ambitious people who are in a hurry to move up. That causes a lot of dissatisfied assistants and high turnover. Entry-level positions open up pretty often, but competition is stiff for the jobs and once you've gotten in you my wish you hadn't.

If you are sure you want to try publishing, here is some advice about actually getting the first job:

1) Try to arrange freelance work, volunteer work for a publishing organization or an internship (which probably won't be paid).

2) Talk to young people in the industry as well as established people. The younger ones have more time to talk (and feel good when they can give advice rather than take orders), more up-to-date job-hunting advice, friends who just might be leaving their entry-level positions imminently, and access to their company's weekly job listings.

3) Learn to type (at least 55 wpm). All editorial jobs require it and lack of typing skills is a stupid reason to be turned down for a job. Besides, once you have a job, the less time you spend typing and retyping, the more time you can spend on more interesting work.

4) Make it clear to perspective employers that you have a realistic idea of the amount of drudgery involved and that you still want the job. Employers don't want to hire someone who is going to be disillusioned within a month and quit, or be miserable.

Good luck!

Bibliography

Books

Books, The Culture and Commerce of Publishing, Lewis Coser, Charles Kadushin and Walter Powell, Basic Books, New York, New York, 1982.
A basic textbook and guide to the book business. Gives an insight to corporate culture.

The Children's Picture Book, Ellen Roberts, Writer's Digest Books, Cincinnati, Ohio, 1981.
Everything you need to know about how children's books are made, from manuscript to bound book.

Creative Careers, Gary Blake and Robert Bly, Wiley Press, New York, 1983.
Excellent descriptive chapter on book publishing. Very good bibliography.

Inside Track, Ross and Kathryn Petras, Vintage Books, New York, 1986.
Focuses on individual companies, some in publishing, including Harper & Row, Random House, and Simon & Schuster.

Opportunities in Book Publishing, John Tebbel, VGM Career Horizons, Skokie, Illinois, 1979.
Good basic description of the industry and the available jobs.

What Happens in Book Publishing, Chandler Grannis, Columbia University Press, New York, New York, 1967.
An in-depth view of the book business by one of the industry experts. A good book for the varsity job hunter.

Directories

1989 Internships, F&W Publications, Cincinnati, Ohio, annual.
Describes internships and summer jobs in book publishing, along with other categories. Eligibility and application information for each listing.

The Book Publishing Annual, R.R. Bowker Co., New York, New York, annual.
Industry news and statistics. Good way to get an overview of how the industry is doing and why. Read this before you go on any interviews.

Book Publishing Career Directory, Career Publishing Corporation, New York, New York, 1985.
Excellent resource. Includes articles by industry

Book Publishing

professionals on every aspect of publishing. Also, has great listings of entry-level employers, training programs, internships. Begin your research here.

Getting Work Experience, Betsy Bauer, Dell Publishing, New York, New York, 1985.
Among other listings, describes summer internship programs in television and film. Gives pertinent application information including pay scales (if any), qualifications desired, and deadlines.

Guide to Book Publishing Courses, Susan Shaffer, Peterson's Guides, Princeton, New Jersey, 1979.
If you would like a slight edge on the competition, you might want to invest in a publishing course. This guide will give you all the options.

Literary Market Place, R.R. Bowker Co., New York, New York, annual.
The industry directory. Lists all major U.S. publishers with subject and activity indexes. Also has a good list of services connected with the industry (freelance editing service, literary agencies, etc.). Use this directory for your preliminary list making.

The Student Guide to Mass Media Internships, Vol. 1, Ronald Claxton, Intern Research Group, University of Colorado, Boulder, Colorado, annual.
Lists internships available in publishing (and other areas) with requirements, pay scales and deadlines.

Writer's Market, Writer's Digest Books, Cincinnati, Ohio, annual.
Lists major publishers with addresses, phone numbers, editor's name and a description of the types of manuscript they are willing to review. Use this directory with the LMP to get good basic background on individual publishers.

Periodicals

Publishers Weekly, R.R. Bowker, New York, New York, weekly. The industry trade magazine.

Chapter 6

Magazine Publishing

Too many people forget that at the core of the magazine business are still great headlines, great cover lines, great photography, great illustration, great positioning, wonderful writing, and after all that is done, great promotion and great salesmanship. That's what we choose to do with that pile of paper -- make something really good.
- Peter G. Diamandis, President, CBS Magazines[1]

The magazine industry is alive and well in the late 80's and is expected to continue that way in the foreseeable future. You would think in the age of the personal computer, cable TV, and VCR's that people could find other media to hold their attention much more effectively than the magazine. However, the fact is that the new technology is not yet well enough developed to replace the magazine. Magazines are less expensive to produce, more portable, easier to use, and more attractive than any comparable technological medium.

Industry Profile

According to 1986 industry statistics, there were 11,328 different periodicals published in the United States, an increase of 238 from 1985.[2] These periodicals fall into variety of classifications. However, the majority can be classified into four basic areas.

---

[1]*Magazine Publishing Career Directory* 1986.

[2]*The 1986 IMS Directory of Publications*

137

Consumer Magazines

Consumer magazines are those directed to the general public. Major ones, such as *The New Yorker, Cosmopolitan,* and *People,* are called the "slicks" because of their slick paper stock. These magazines, many of which are headquartered in New York City and Chicago, are very popular places to work, and the competition is keen for entry-level jobs. Also included in this category are specialized publications aimed at a limited portion of the general public having a common interest or viewpoint, such as, *Golfers Digest, Gourmet,* and *Bride.*

As a part of the consumer magazine segment, there are also "little" publications which include independent journals of poetry, fiction, and commentary. They are often financially supported by devotees of pure literature.

Trade, Technical and Professional Magazines

Trade publications serve a specific field or function in business, industry or the professions. Business people rely on these magazines to bring them up-to-date on the changes and developments within their industry. The average trade magazine has a circulation of from 40 to 75,000.

The typical trade journal has the sale of advertising space as its primary source of income, with manufacturers currently investing over a billion dollars annually in advertising preparation and buying space. Major trade journals have circulations in the hundreds of thousands. A trade journal may have a staff of as many as 40 people. The news content, which consists primarily of specialized articles, how-to features and industry social news, is usually staff-written, and the writers and editors either have a personal background in the particular field or are journalists who are trained in-house.

Sponsored Publications

Sponsored publications are those that are produced by business firms, unions, associations or institutions. Company publications, often called house magazines, can be divided into two categories. They are called "internals" if they are written primarily for employees of a company, and "externals" if they are produced for a group such as stockholders or customers.

A house magazine is not the same thing as a trade magazine. A trade magazine reports on an entire industry or field, and a house magazine deals only with a particular company and any industry news pertaining directly to it. Another difference is that trade papers are business ventures which make money from advertising and subscriptions, while house magazines are generally free and have no advertising. There are many thousands of house magazines published and the most comprehensive directory is the *Internal Publications Directory*.

Sunday Supplement Magazines

Many city and regional newspapers publish weekly Sunday magazines which include general interest material. The articles usually relate to the particular city, state or region in which the magazine appears. A notable exception is *Parade*, which is national, added to many Sunday newspapers throughout the country. The staff of a regional Sunday magazine is usually small, numbering around four to ten, although larger publications may have an editorial staff of 20 or more. A listing of some of the Sunday supplements can be found in *Literary Market Place*.

Career Profiles

Those types of positions special to the magazine industry fall into six categories, including editorial, design, advertising sales, production, promotion, and circulation.

Editorial

The editorial office of a magazine is the creative center of the business. The content of the entire magazine falls under the direction of the chief editorial staff members. The editorial department produces editorials and columns, assigns articles to staff writers, and selects freelance material from outside writers. The editorial department holds meetings to discuss each issue, plan the table of contents, select the cover picture, and many other content-related tasks.

Depending upon the size of the publication, there may be many editors on the staff, or there many be only one. Titles and responsibilities vary. A quick rundown of the titles in the editorial department will give you an idea of the different functions: editor, editorial director, executive editor, copy editor, national editor, literary editor, roving editor, editorial manager, senior editor, associate editor, assistant editor, editorial assistant, and contributing editor.

Often an editor will write articles for his department as well as select them from freelancers. Some publications have staff writers who write most of the articles, essays, and reviews. Typically, the smaller the editorial staff, the more dependent the publication is on freelancers to contribute articles. A magazine may have a stable of freelancers who submit articles on a regular basis, often at the suggestion of the editorial staff.

Writing vs. Editing

Those interested exclusively in writing should carefully review potential employers to see how much of the material is written by editors versus outside or in-house staff writers. Becoming a staff writer usually requires a stint as a freelancer or newspaper journalist/reporter. Magazines hire staff writers after the writer has established a reputation or style that the magazine wants for its exclusive use. It is difficult to make a transition from editor to staff writer. Therefore, if you want to be a writer, you may not want to become an editor. Read some of the books mentioned in the bibliography about getting started as a writer.

Entry-level jobs in the editorial department include editorial assistant, copyeditor, picture editor, and researcher. All require a certain amount of clerical/secretarial tasks, including typing, filing, and proofreading.

Design

The design department is concerned primarily with the "look" of the "book" (the industry term for `magazine'). The design department creates the consistent, overall design of the magazine. It decides on the different typefaces, the format, and the paper quality.

Jobs in the design department are, obviously, closely linked to those in editorial because the content many times influences the design. Positions within the art department include art director, associate art director, assistant art director, art associate, and graphic designer.

The entry-level position in the design department of a magazine usually is as a graphic artist. Your job is to assist the senior designers and complete many of the design ideas they create. Therefore, your job may include a good deal of paste-up and layout work. As you become familiar with the design of a particular magazine, you will be given responsibility for different sections of the magazine.

Production

The production department is in charge of the physical manufacture of the magazine, from typesetting the copy, to ordering paper, to printing and binding the magazine, and finally, to getting the magazine to its point of sale. Naturally, this department must work closely with the design department. In fact, many people in production have design experience or training.

Different divisions within this department include traffic, makeup, scheduling, purchasing, and cost control, and each division has its hierarchy of positions. The Production Manager is the top position in most magazines.

Production of a large, full-color, nationally distributed magazine involves a highly sophisticated technology. Knowledge of the latest typesetting, printing and binding techniques is essential. Bringing out an issue in a timely and economical fashion determines the final profit picture for the business as a whole. It is estimated that 50 percent of the cost of publishing a magazine goes towards it production. Therefore, those who like the details of producing the best possible product for the least amount of money will enjoy the rewards of a career in production.

Advertising Sales, Circulation, and Promotion

These departments are combined here because the primary function in each department is to sell. The advertising sales department sells space to advertisers, who are usually the principal monetary supporters of a publication. The circulation department sells to the consumer and is responsible for increasing subscriptions yearly through direct mail campaigns and media promotions. The promotions department also works to promote the sale of the magazine, both to consumers and advertisers, by getting the publication into the public eye. They send press releases to the media, publicizing features and/or writers.

Looking at the masthead (usually on the third or fourth page of the magazine) of one major consumer publication, you will see that the top jobs in these areas are: advertising director, director of single copy sales, circulation manager, direct mail manager, fulfillment manager, circulation production manager, advertising production manager, and promotions manager.

There are usually more opportunities for beginners in these departments than in the editorial department. Typical entry-level jobs are: market research analyst, circulation development assistant, promotion copywriter, and sales representative. The routes through the circulation and advertising sales department often lead to the top positions in a publishing company. In general, a knowledge of the marketing aspects of selling a magazine will be an asset to your career.

Salary

As with most jobs in media, starting salaries in magazine publishing are around $20,000. Most begin in the mid teens, depending upon the department. Sales jobs will reap the highest salaries when commission is figured into the formula. Jobs in editorial are on the low end, sometimes starting below $13,000. Your chances for getting a better wage are greater at magazines that are part of magazine groups such as Hearst or Conde Nast.

In upper level management positions you can expect to earn a respectable living. However, as with most publishing jobs (books, newspapers) high six-figure salaries are a rarity.

Job-Hunting Tips

Finding a job in magazine publishing depends a great deal upon which aspect of the business you wish to enter. Jobs in the editorial department require one kind of approach, those in design require another, and those in the other departments require yet another approach. However, hunting for any job in magazines requires a background and enthusiasm for the printed word. You must be the kind of person who loves to pick up, look at, and read magazines. If you have fun just browsing through your local newsstand, then you are probably a good candidate for the magazine business.

Start reading *Folio*, the industry trade magazine. It is directed towards the business side of magazines, but it will give you an inside view of the concerns and the vocabulary of the industry. Read general descriptive material on the magazine industry. The best introduction to the industry is the *Magazine Publishing Career Directory* by the Career Publishing Corporation.

Use the *Magazine Industry Marketplace*, *Writers Market*, and the *Gale Directory* to put together a comprehensive list of magazines that interest you. It is important to include magazines of all sizes and types in order to increase your chances of finding an entry-level opportunity.

Of course, you should limit your list to those publications that appear to be within your own interest areas. You have to be sincerely enthusiastic about working for

144

the publications on your list. So, if you can't see yourself covering news about golf, cross out *Golfers Digest!*

The next step is to compile a list of potential contacts within the field. Read the Introduction for a strategy to tackle this task.

Getting Experience

If magazine publishing seems to be the career for you, try to get some experience on a campus publication. Summer internships are available at many of the major consumer publications. Get involved in any kind of publishing project.

Are you interested in the design aspect? You will have to create a portfolio of sample layouts and designs for publications you designed. (Most people in design have a technical background and training in graphic arts, but it is not impossible for someone in liberal arts to break in with strong extracurricular experience.)

Those interested in the editorial and the business side of magazine publishing should get involved in the creation of a new publication or the ongoing operations of an existing publication. Any experience editing, proofing, copyediting, dealing with circulation problems, production, etc. will be invaluable.

Writers should get experience working on a newspaper or magazine where you will be able to write feature-length stories, reviews, investigative reports, and other well-developed pieces. Try to have at least ten examples of your best writing ready to show editors. Also, read Chapter 3 on print journalism for more job-hunting ideas.

Getting the First Job

Make your contact with potential employers as specific as possible. Indicate for which area of the magazine you would like to work, indicate your ultimate goal, and be creative. Your letter to the managing editor or the manager of whichever department attracts you, should be interesting to read and it should make the person want to meet you. Ask for advice, not a job. Your goal is to meet as many people in the magazine business as you can in order to uncover as many leads and opportunities as possible.

Your resume should have a section entitled "Publishing Experience" in which you list all related experience, paid or unpaid, you have had in publishing. Give the reader the impression that you have a specific career goal in mind.

If you are interested in editing or writing, you should include five or six writing samples. If you were responsible for publishing a magazine on campus, send a copy of your best issue.

A final important note: before you talk with anyone in the magazine industry, read and study his or her publication! Never go into a meeting or interview without at least a basic understanding of what your interviewer spends ten or more hours a day of his or her life doing!!

Case Study

Parker Reilly, Assistant Editor

Parker Reilly is assistant to the Senior Editor at Cosmopolitan. He is also the cartoon editor and he writes the "People"

146

page. Parker was a government concentrator with no particular publishing experience as an undergraduate, but had a keen interest in magazines.

After graduating from college with a bachelor's degree in English and American literature, I went to work as a press secretary on a congressional campaign (I had previously worked for this congressman as a campaign volunteer and caseworker during a year off from school).

Unfortunately, we lost the election, and I suddenly found myself unemployed. After a soul-searching time spent rethinking my career goals (read: waiting tables), I decided the time had come to find another job. My experiences writing and disseminating press releases, as well as my overall contact with the print media, made me realize that I would like my next career position to be in publishing. I went to the Office of Career Services for some information, as I didn't even know the name of the position I desired. As it turned out, "editorial assistant" seemed to be what I was looking for; now I had only to land a job.

I relocated to New York City. As well as being my original home, it was also, conveniently, the center of the industry in which I was interested. My first step was to make a list of not only all the publishing people I knew, but of all the other professionals I knew as well. These included personal friends, family friends, and a few friends-of-friends. I did not expect any of these people to offer me a job directly; what I did want from them were their ideas on job hunting, as well as the names of any publishing people they might know who would know of job openings.

The ensuing conversations were invaluable to me in several ways: first of all, they were good practice for the actual interviews that laid ahead. I found myself becoming more composed after each conversation, as well as increasingly familiar with my own career goals and personal attributes (and better able to communicate these in a way that straddled the line between overbearing boasting and impractical humbleness). Also, these contacts invariably knew at least one person in my chosen field, generally someone who was in a high position. Let's face it -- it's much better to have a managing editor as a contact than someone's cousin who works in the mail room. Who's more likely to be able to offer you a job?

After each conversation, I would send out what amounted to a thank-you note. These are a good idea because these contacts are busy people and the gift of their time and experience is a valuable gift indeed. Also, it's important to maintain your network of professional contacts. These people can become friends whom you may wish to consult at times during the course of your own professional life, and it's important for them to remember your name and remember it with a positive association. I can think of two such people whom I met in the course of my job search and whom I see at least every other month, keeping them apprised of my career status and just generally shooting the breeze. Remember, this is most certainly not the last job you will have to find for yourself.

The next phase of my job search was the actual interview process. My first stop was at the personnel offices of two large publishing houses: Hearst and Conde Nast. I had contacts at specific magazines within these houses, but it was important to go the conventional route as well as the more direct route. While it is an individual who will ultimately offer you a job, you will actually be employed by the magazine itself, and they will at least want to think that they had a hand in hiring you.

At this point the rejections began. Some frequently heard statements: "You are so great that I wish I could create a job for you, but we simply have no openings;" or "This is the best resume since Edward R. Murrow's, but I'm afraid you can't type fast enough;" or the ego-bolstering, "We have people with ten years experience who would give their right arm for a position in our letters department, so, if you would be so kind, take a hike." Responses ranged from friendly and encouraging to disinterested and downright impolite, but the bottom line was, I still had no job.

Then I got lucky. A friend who knew I was looking, and who herself worked in the industry, told me of an opening (in fact two) at her magazine. After a friendly interview (during which I was actually relaxed enough to make a joke, something about Mother Theresa making more yearly than I would be taking home), and a week of waiting, I got the job. My search had taken almost three months, but I had wound up with a job that was exactly what I wanted.

A few final thoughts . . . When I say luck played a part in my ultimate employment, I meant it. So when looking for that first job, it's important to improve your chances for a lucky break as much as possible. Get your name around, talk to anyone you can think of with even the vaguest connection to your industry of choice. Many of these kinds of jobs are filled through personal referrals, and rarely through want-ads or even that magazine's personnel department. It is vital to keep alert for actual openings. If you do hear of an opening -- ATTACK! Treat it (assuming you do want that job) as if it's the last opening on earth. It may well be.

Bibliography

Books for Future Writers

1001 Article Ideas, Frank A. Dickson, Writers Digest Books, Cincinnati, Ohio, 1979.

This book acts as a coach and cheerleading squad for those interested in making a living as a freelance writer by suggesting starting places for articles.

The Business of Being a Writer, Stephen Goldin and Kathleen Sky, Harper & Row, New York, New York, 1982.

Gets down to the details of fending for yourself in the publishing world. Gives advice on submissions, contracts, and other presentation and negotiation techniques.

How to Get Happily Published, Judith Appelbaum and Nancy Evans, Harper & Row, New York, New York, 1978.

An introduction to the subtleties of getting your writing published. Interesting information from an insider's point of view about the publishing industry.

Jobs for Writers, Kirk Polking, Editor, Writer's Digest Books, Cincinnati, Ohio, 1980.

Describes many different types of jobs in which writing is a key component. Read this book to get an insight to the range of possibilities for the would-be writer.

Books for Future Editors and Publishers

Inside Track, Ross and Kathryn Petras, Vintage Books, New York, New York, 1986.

To get a feel for what it's like to work for Conde Nast, Time, People, and Sports Illustrated read the chapter on magazines. It also has good descriptive information on specific careers within each company.

Opportunities in Magazine Publishing, John Tebbel, VGM Career Horizons, Skokie, Illinois, 1980.
Gives a good basic outline of the magazine business. Skim through this book to help you identify areas of interest and then find greater detail in other sources.

Directories

1989 Internships, Lisa Hulse, Editor, Writer's Digest Books, Cincinnati, Ohio, annual.
Lists a collection of paid and volunteer magazine internships. A good source for summer jobs.

Getting Work Experience, Betsy Bauer, Dell Publishing, New York, New York, 1985.
Lists a collection of paid and volunteer magazine internships. A good source for summer jobs when combined with 1987 Internships and the Mass Media Internship guides.

Hudson's Newsletter Directory, Margaret Leonard, Editor, Rhinebeck, New York, annual.
For another way to employ your writing and editing skills you should look here for a long list of (mostly) in-house newsletters.

Gale Directory of Publications, Gale Research, Inc., Fort Washington, Pennsylvania, annual.
One of the most comprehensive guides to publishing. Organized by state and city, this directory gives a detailed listing of every newspaper, magazine, newsletter published in each locale with names, addresses, phone numbers, and descriptions. Also has a series of subject-oriented indexes. This directory will help you to compile a long list of potential employers.

Magazine Industry Market Place, R.R. Bowker, New York, New York, annual. A directory of the magazine industry. Not as comprehensive as the IMS Directory, but more detailed. Use this directory along with the Writer's Market and IMS to complete your prospect list.

Magazine Publishing Career Directory, Career Publishing Corporation, New York, New York, 1986. An excellent guide to the industry. The main section of the directory contains articles by industry professionals on different aspects of magazine publishing. The remaining sections provide lists of potential employers, training programs, internships, etc. Don't miss this one.

The New York Writer's Source Book, Department of Cultural Affairs, Addison Wesley, Reading, Massachusetts, 1983. Provides tips and sources for those trying to make a living as writers in New York.

The Student Guide to Mass Media Internships, Intern Research Group, University of Colorado, Boulder, Colorado, annual. Lists a collection of paid and volunteer magazine internships. A good source for summer jobs.

Writer's Market, Paula Deimling, Editor, Writer's Digest Books, Cincinnati, Ohio, annual. An excellent source of information for the writer and job hunter. Gives details about hundreds of magazines, including editor's name, type and style of submissions, and specific articles about jobs and people in magazines.

Chapter 7

Advertising

> *Do agencies really want or need people with "street smarts" who have learned to survive independently and view openness and trust with caution, even cynicism? Egoists out to "win through intimidation" while they "look out for Number One?" Hustlers ready to trick the buying public at every turn? I don't think so. In fact, I think what the industry has always had and needs more of are humanists. Humanists are team players, people capable of working with other people and for other people. Advertising agency professionals work with others at the client companies and, ultimately, for the general public.*
> *- Harry Clark, Senior V.P., JWT Company[1]*

Advertising Age, the industry's leading trade magazine, reports that the top 500 advertising agencies have grown in the last ten years from a $12 billion enterprise to one netting over $41 billion.[2] For an industry that has been typecast as unstable, this statistic gives advertising a new image. Even through the recession years of the late 70's and early 80's, advertising continued to grow the in face of double-digit inflation.

You would think that jobs would be plentiful because of such success. However, advertising continues to be a very competitive job market for most applicants. An ad agency's success depends on keeping overhead costs to a minimum and the staff small. Also, because of the fast-paced environment, most agencies haven't had time to develop training programs or recruiting strategies. The dynamic nature of advertising makes job hunting a challenge. Like many of the other media industries, it pays to know a good deal about it before looking for a job.

---

[1] *Advertising Career Directory*
[2] *Advertising Age,* March 27, 1986.

Industry Profile

Every ongoing business concern, private or public, profit or non-profit, has some kind of advertising function. Therefore, to profile advertising is to see advertising in many different contexts.

In-House Advertising

Businesses which spend a great deal of money on advertising sometimes set up their own agencies "in-house." These in-house departments are fully staffed and function like an independent agency, but they are on the company payroll. Procter & Gamble is an example of a large manufacturer with a well-established and high-quality in-house advertising department.

However, most businesses do not have in-house agencies. They have advertising departments which oversee the company's general advertising policies. An advertising manager might head the department and be responsible for planning and presenting an advertising budget to the board of directors. The manager would then hire an independent agency, explain what the company wanted to sell, and how much money could be spent. He would continue acting as liaison between the company and the ad agency.

Department stores, unlike most other businesses, often have large, fully-staffed, in-house agencies because of the large amount of advertising they do. The in-house staff is often responsible for designing, producing, and buying space for all the print advertising that appears. Most retailers, however, hire outside agencies to handle the non-print (TV and radio) advertising.

The Media

Radio and television stations, newspapers and maga-

154

zines, etc., also have advertising staffs. These departments not only sell space or time to advertisers, but they also create advertising, often for small and/or local organizations. The advertising salesperson, as the representative of the station or publication, tries to convince advertisers that his or her medium is the appropriate one for their campaign.

The advertising salesperson deals with media buyers and account executives in an advertising agency and with the advertising manager on the client side. Because of this close interaction, job crossover is frequent with advertising sales reps moving into agencies in either account work or media buying, or joining the advertising departments of former corporate buyers. Advertising can also be a starting off point for those interested in working in television.

Advertising Suppliers

Advertising departments and advertising agencies, especially smaller ones, often rely on a variety of firms which specialize in different advertising functions. There are jobs similar to those in an agency in the following firms: media service organizations; direct mail agencies; sales promotion agencies; typographers; market research firms; and film and videotape houses.

Advertising Agencies

An advertising agency is a consulting firm which plans, creates, prepares, and places advertising for its clients. Most agencies are paid on a commission system in which the agency keeps a percentage of the cost of the space or time that they buy for their clients; a small percentage of companies are paid on the fee system.

There are more than 5000 agencies in the United States with the heaviest concentration in New York City where most of the largest firms are headquartered, and Chicago, the second largest market area.

Agency Organization

To get an idea of the different jobs available within advertising, you must have an understanding of how an advertising agency or ad department works. Each agency has two major functions, client services and creative services. Within most agencies there is a clear division between the two aspects of agency work and once your career begins in one area there is little opportunity to switch. Therefore, it becomes important to decide early on which side of the advertising business intrigues you most.

Client services is the liaison between the agency and the advertiser. The people involved in client services are primarily responsible for organizing an advertising campaign for an advertiser.

Creative services is the department responsible for actually creating the idea or concept for the advertising campaign and seeing that concept through to a finished product. The creative department creates and produces the advertisements and commercials for magazines, newspapers, billboards, TV and radio. Some large agencies also have sales promotion departments which produce other advertising material, such as booklets, mailers, signs, window displays, catalogues, sales kits, etc.

Career Profiles

Client Services

The account executive is the link between the agency and the client. With the client, an account executive (AE) determines the marketing problem or advertising goal. The AE must then research the product or service, including its competition, the markets, distribution, etc.

This material is presented to the management team in the agency and a general strategy is established. The AE coordinates the various agency departments in developing the marketing plan into a specific advertising program.

Working as a team with other agency representatives, the AE is responsible for presenting the completed advertising program to client management. An AE must have good analytical skills to do the marketing, competitive analysis, and strategic planning; he or she must have good management skills to coordinate the various agency departments in the development of the advertising program.

An AE, finally, must have good sales skills in getting the program accepted by the client. There are usually frequent meetings prior to approval, but once the advertising program has been accepted, the AE oversees the implementation. For example, this could entail "going on a shoot" along with the creative people, ensuring the smooth production of a commercial.

A few agencies will hire B.A.'s as assistant account executives or bring them into a training program designed to give them enough experience to become assistant account executives in six months to two years.

Some agencies place trainees directly on an account under the direction of an account manager, with responsibilities ranging from interpretation of market research data and testing or positioning new products, to developing media strategy, or evaluating the effect of government regulations on client business. These trainees are also given exposure to the service departments, such as media, traffic, production, and public relations; and they sometimes participate in departmental presentations.

Most agencies, however, place the BA's directly into one of the service departments, such as media or market research, for 12-18 months, at the end of which they become either assistant AE's or full-fledged account executives. Many of the smaller agencies don't have assistant account executives.

Depending upon the particular program and individual performance, an assistant AE might be promoted to account executive in from eight to eighteen months. A full account executive has responsibility for the management of one account, often a brand or product of a client. After two to six years, an AE could be promoted to account supervisor, responsible for one or more accounts and the supervision of several AE's.

Most agencies have a market research department responsible for determining who the buyers are -- their behavior and attitudes. Research is done on specific products to find out if they meet consumer expectations. It is also done on the copy to find out if people are motivated by the advertising. A market research assistant would be involved in gathering the data for these studies and doing preliminary analysis. This is a common entry point for many liberal arts graduates.

The media department is another entry spot for recent graduates. The media department's responsibility is to ensure that the advertising reaches the appropriate audience. It determines, via research and judgement, the best media for the client to use. The costs of buying advertising space and broadcast time have increased substantially in the last decade, and the growth in size and responsibility of the media department has been one result. A good media plan can have a significant impact on product sales.

There are three subdivisions within the media department: research, planning, and buying. The media researcher gathers and analyzes data on the media, the demographics of the people who are exposed to the different media, and the impact and believability of advertising in different media environments. The planning department, usually the largest area, looks at the numbers and then, relying on past experience, good judgement and creativity, prepares a media plan and schedule. The media planner must then sell the plan to the AE and the client.

The media buyer negotiates directly with the media and must learn how to deal effectively with media salespeople. Good bargaining skills are essential. People in this division get guarantees on the preemptibility of their ads and check that ads are run in the correct place or time slots.

The entry-level jobs in the media department can involve tedious number crunching. There is usually a lot of work at the computer terminal. It takes from one to two years for a new buyer to operate without close supervision. With experience, people get more supervisory responsibility becoming space-buying group heads, assistant directors and directors. Many media assistants try to break into account management as assistant AE's after a year's experience.

Another entry point leading to the account executive slot is in traffic. The traffic department keeps all the agency departments operating on schedule. This group follows the ad through the creative department and sees that all internal deadlines are met. It makes sure that the printing and reproduction materials, electrical transcriptions for radio spots, and tapes for TV commercials are prepared, submitted to the client for approval, and sent to the appropriate media by their deadline. Because it provides an opportunity to become familiar with all the agency departments and their functions, traffic can be a good training ground.

"Creative"

The copywriter and art director (AD) are the creative forces behind the advertising campaign. As a team, they come up with the concept for the campaign, write, design and supervise the production of the advertising.

The copywriter must first and foremost be able to write easily and well under pressure. He or she might begin by studying the consumer and product research data and, from there, write an ad that speaks directly to the individual consumer. In any case, the writing must be new, fresh, and always effective. The challenge for the writer is to keep the ideas flowing year after year.

A junior copywriter might begin by writing ads for trade publications and/or body copy for packages under the supervision of a senior writer. A large agency usually requires about two years of experience from copywriters before they can work on television ads.

The career path of a writer leads from junior to senior writer. Copy group head, copy supervisor, and creative supervisor or director are increasingly responsible positions. Career satisfaction, however, often comes from recognition of good work rather than promotions. There are many industry awards for the top creative work each year.

The art director works closely with the copywriter to design a successful ad. The AD's primary responsibility is to visualize the ad in several different ways in different media. Art directors may not be exceptional artists, but they must have some technical knowledge of design, graphics, typography, and photography. An art director rarely creates the finished artwork for an ad. The emphasis here is on "direction."

AD's oversee the visual side of the ad from layout to

finished product. They select artists and photographers to work on the ad, and in film they get involved in all the components of a commercial, from casting talent to the selection of film technique.

A junior art director might begin in an agency working in the "bullpen" doing paste-ups and mechanicals for a number of accounts. Assistant art directors gain more responsibility and begin to contribute to the creation of the "concept." The career of an art director often parallels that of the writer. Often the most talented creative people combine their efforts with their friends on the client services side and start their own agencies.

You begin to realize why so many agencies have such long names! In the process of creating a television commercial, the creative team develops a "storyboard" showing the sequence of scenes in the ad along with the copy. In the realization of the storyboard, the copywriter and art director work with a third person -- the producer -- who coordinates the production elements before filming or taping.

The agency producer has a part in selecting the outside production company (usually consisting of the director and film crew) and is the person primarily responsible for bringing the production in on budget. The producer must be familiar with all the technical aspects of making a commercial because he or she must evaluate all the work being done. Producers may begin as assistants and usually have had substantial filmmaking experience.

Salary

Depending upon the size of the agency, assistant account executives usually earn $20,00 or more. Those on the creative side should probably expect 10% to 15% less.

Jobs in media, traffic, and research may expect less. However, once you have made a name for yourself and proven your worth, a $35 to $40,000 paycheck is not unusual after just a few years. The amount goes up from there depending on your talent and the agency's success. Top level creative and management executives often make six-figure salaries.

Job-Hunting Tips

Job hunting is especially challenging in the advertising industry because you are making a presentation of yourself to people who are the experts at presentation. It becomes essential, therefore, to prepare as best you can for the challenge.

Begin your preparation by becoming an advertising fanatic. Collect ads that you love and hate. Start a advertising notebook chronicling your view of advertising. At some point, you should begin to form a philosophy of what you think makes good advertising. Those interviewing you for jobs will be interested in how you view the industry, having had no or little experience.

At the same time, read, read, read . . . any books on advertising you can find. Do not miss reading any books by David Ogilvy, especially *Confessions of an Advertising Man*. *How to Get a Job in Advertising* by Ken Haas is an excellent and straightforward guide to the ad game. The *Advertising Career Directory* published by Career Publishing Inc. is an excellent overview of the industry. *30 Seconds* by Michael Arlen is an insightful and humorous look at the creative side of the business. Many of the books about advertising are by industry professionals and are more memoirs than objective descriptions. However, the American Association of Advertising Agencies does publish a short guide that gives a clear definition of the industry, entitled *Advertising, a Guide to Careers in Advertising.*

Once you think you have a good grasp of what happens in advertising, start reading *Advertising Age* magazine, the industry trade publication. *Ad Age*, as it's often called, covers all the news of the industry, including prize winners, mergers, trends, innovations, etc. Reading this one magazine is probably the most important reading you can do in preparation for the job hunt. It will introduce you to the vocabulary of the industry and allow you to "speak the language" in interviews. Other important reading includes *Ad Week* and *Ad East.*

Once you have "studied" the industry, you should think about ways to get some firsthand experience to help you decide which aspect of advertising interests you most.

Getting Experience

It is very important that you gain some exposure to a professional ad agency and experience what it's like to work in a hectic, fast-paced, and often nerve-wracking business. Term-time internships are the best way to gain this exposure. Volunteer 15 hours a week for a semester and you will find out whether advertising is something you would like to pursue. If you can, work for both a small (under 50 employees) and a large agency (more than 200 employees).

The time spent in an internship will be well worthwhile, not only for the experience, but also for the people you will meet. Often, an internship can lead to a full-time job at your agency or through a contact from someone for whom you have worked. Because so many agencies do not have formal training programs, their interns become logical entry-level candidates. If you are interested in taking a leave to gain this type of experience, check *The Standard Directory of Advertising Agencies* (The Red Book) for a complete listing of all recognized ad agencies in the country. This directory has an excellent geographic index to help you identify appropriate agencies.

Summer work in ad agencies is also a good way to gain experience. However, many agencies don't pay their interns, so this option is often impractical. Nevertheless, if you can create a situation where you work part-time for an agency and part-time in a paying job, this option becomes more realistic.

Other valuable experience can be gained by working for student organizations. Volunteer to help publicize an event or service, become the advertising manager for a publication... in fact, any position which allows you to demonstrate your leadership, organizational, and/or creative abilities is good preparation for a career in advertising.

Putting Your Book Together

To begin job hunting for a job on the creative side, you must create a portfolio (book) of your best advertising ideas. Your book should present about six concepts in a variety of media: print ads, billboards, radio and television commercials. You can take an existing ad and redo it to your standards. Or, try inventing a product and creating a series of ads for it. If you are challenged and enjoy putting together 20 to 30 sample ads, you will probably enjoy working on the creative side of advertising.

If you want to be a copywriter, it is obvious that you should put your emphasis on the copy, but you should also include a rough sketch or, at least, indications of how you envision the graphics. The opposite is true for future art directors; put your emphasis on the visuals, but include some copy. To help you with this arduous task, read *How to Put Your Book Together and Get a Job in Advertising* by Maxine Paetro.

Don't be too concerned about a professional looking book; your ideas are the important thing. Naturally, the better your book looks, the better the ideas come across, so if you have the ability to create polished material, do so. If possible, with the help of career advisers, get an objective, professional critique of your book before braving the job market.

Getting the First Job

With experience and knowledge, you will be ready to successfully confront the advertising job market. Start by assembling your list of target agencies or companies. Use the *Red Book* and the *Standard Directory of Advertisers* to assemble your list. Note that both directories reveal a great deal of information about the particular company. For ad agencies, knowing their client list is very important. For every agency on your list, try to get some samples of their advertising for your advertising notebook. Also, the directories will have the most recent names of key executives. It is very important to address your cover letters to a specific person.

If you are looking for a job on the client services side of the business, create a resume which highlights your advertising experience and other experience which demonstrates your organizational, leadership, and analytical talents.

On the creative side, your resume should outline any technical experience you have had in graphics, video, or other media. You have the option of being very creative with your resume by designing it in an unusual, offbeat way. Some creatives write an ad for themselves in place of a resume. In any case, your resume will merely be an introduction to your book.

Next, assemble your list of contacts in advertising. Internship directors, faculty advisers, alumni contacts, and family contacts are good people to head your list. Visit these people first to get advice on your target list, resume, and book.

Write individual cover letters to each of your target agencies. Don't do a mass mailing! Start with 10 or 12 letters. This will allow you to put more emphasis on your letter and to follow up on each more effectively. Your cover letter should be exceptional. Write several drafts making sure to avoid any cliches or standard phrasing. Read the chapter on letters in *Executive Jobs Unlimited* by Carl Boll to get an idea of how an effective letter is written.

Be prepared to visit many people in your search. For "creatives," you will have to leave your book for several days for consideration. If possible, make several copies so that you can speed up your search. The more people you visit, the sooner an opportunity will arise. Be persistent.

New York vs. The Rest of the World

One large question for most job hunters is whether or not to begin their advertising careers in New York. There are several opinions on this score. Your decision should be based largely on what your ultimate goals are.

New York is the center of the advertising industry. Therefore, if you want to be in the thick of national and international advertising, you will have to spend some time in New York. There are a few exceptions to this rule, but they are very few. For those interested in television, keep in mind that most of the high-quality commercials are produced (not necessarily shot) in New York.

Also, "New York Experience" is very valuable when you want to leave New York. So, if you hate New York, perhaps you can live with the idea of going there for one or two years because of the boost it will give your career.

However, if you are not interested in national advertising, your geographic options are limitless. Every major city in the nation has an active advertising community. Also, if you decide ultimately that New York is your goal, experience in a smaller city agency will certainly help you.

Deciding whether to work for a small or large agency is much the same question as whether or not to work in New York. A large agency with more clients has greater diversity. You are exposed to more types of accounts. However, you may not have the kind of responsibilities that you would have at a smaller agency. Many people suggest starting in a smaller agency to learn the fundamentals of the business and then moving on to a larger agency to gain exposure to larger regional or national accounts.

Ultimately, the most important factor in your first job becomes the one person who supervises your work. If your boss cares about your development as a professional and takes the time to teach you the ropes, it won't really matter in which agency you work, large or small. A good working relationship can lead to more career success than almost any other factor. Of course, it is even more helpful if your boss is a talented advertising executive because you might benefit from his or her success.

Case Study

Stephanie Moffett, Account Executive

Stephanie was very active in undergraduate extra-curriculars and concentrated in English. She spent one summer working in a small ad agency. She is now an Account Executive at Needham Harper - Worldwide.

I can't really remember when I made the final decision to go into advertising. The only advertising related summer job I had was between my freshman and sophomore year in a two-woman advertising/public relations firm in Denver, Colorado. I was a glorified secretary; I typed, answered phones, and ran errands. While I may have grumbled at some of my menial tasks, I have to admit my boss did give me the opportunity to be thoroughly involved in the agency's business. I was able to attend client meetings, arrange a few press conferences, and write some radio copy.

I got a real sense of what it meant to be in advertising: learning not only what work was required but also learning how to put up with the hectic, somewhat frenzied, pace and the wild personal styles of ad execs. My boss was definitely an eccentric: screaming and yelling at the top of her lungs one minute, while the next she'd be dripping with praise. Whenever she yelled though, she'd apologize. For that I was appreciative because there are people who feel that because they're your superior, they have a right to scream at you. Overall, working for this firm was a wonderful initiation into the advertising industry.

The next few summers I tried to land some internships in the larger New York advertising/public relations firms, but the firms I really wanted to work for didn't pay enough to make living in New York feasible.

As I look back, I wouldn't say that not getting an internship was a critical mistake in my career. I firmly believe if you're good, and you're serious about getting into the business, eventually, you'll get where you want to go. This is not to say it's a cinch to find a job. I know firsthand: it's a tough business to break into.

The major task of finding a permanent job took a lot of my time senior year. Some ad agencies (two my graduating year) recruited on campus. But because I thought it was important to investigate as many options as possible, I didn't limit myself to just these two agencies. So, after I went to Harvard's Office of Career Services to get advice on my resume and cover letter, I began reading *Advertising Age* and the *Red Book* copying addresses and names of personnel managers of the major New York agencies. I sat down and wrote off about 40 letters. That was the easy part; the hardest part was to follow-up the letters with phone calls asking for interviews. Because I didn't know a single person in the business, they were all "cold" calls. I can vividly remember how I dreaded dialing those numbers. I tried to convince myself, "Why was I so scared of a simple call?" "They can't see me." "It's no big deal." But boy, how my stomach would turn. I couldn't rest until that day's allotted series of phone calls were over.

It was so disappointing when the people I called were out or asked me to "call back in an hour." I'd have to go through it all over again. Then of course, there was always the generic response of "we'll get back to you in writing." My only comfort was knowing that I had tried my best to make myself known. I also knew that the last thing I wanted was to be too pushy. Once you lose the favor of the personnel department it's hard to win them back. When you've been in the business for a while, you learn personnel managers remember names; that's their business, so it's important to play it cool. Be interested, not overly aggressive.

As I look back, it was a costly endeavor, the whole job hunting process: the cost for printing my resumes, long distance phone calls, trips to New York. While I know it was all worth it, I recognized the whole process was a struggle, mentally and financially.

Perhaps the most enjoyable aspect of the whole job hunting process was the interviewing. It was a chance to show my interest in advertising. But beyond just showing enthusiasm, I knew I had to convey some sort of knowledge about the industry: what were my favorite commercials, what did I think about the creative idea, how was the product targeted, would I buy it, how would I change the ad?

I knew I had to be smart about answering the standard question: why advertising? The last thing I wanted to do was respond with something like, "oh . . . I like people . . . I like to watch TV . . . it seems interesting." You truly need to convince them that you have some idea of what's out there. Granted, it's difficult to be 100% accurate, because you can never really know what an industry or business is like until you get into it, but try to show a little savvy.

As the 1984 recruiting season was winding down, I was called back for second interviews at Benton & Bowles and Grey Advertising. Both agencies offered me jobs and I chose Grey. I got along quite well with the personnel managers there, and I felt good about the executives I had met.

I was to start on a packaged goods account [one where the product is contained in a designed container] which is the "prescribed way" of starting in the business. It's generally believed that once you've learned the disciplines of advertising on a packaged goods account, you'll forever apply those disciplines to any future account.

Many agencies require packaged goods experience. I personally believe, having been on a few accounts since then, that packaged goods accounts is not the only way to go in this business. I, quite frankly, find the creative on most packaged goods accounts to be a bit dry. However, the training I received on my account was quite good; and for someone who is fresh out of college and doesn't really know advertising, it's an excellent way to learn the ropes.

Grey Advertising didn't have a training program; it was basically "sink or swim." "Stars rise to the top" I was told. Looking back, there's no doubt about it; there was a lot of sinking and swimming. I'll be honest: it was tough. I learned more about managerial skills than I did about advertising. The work itself wasn't terribly difficult; it was the environment and attitude under which I worked: "no matter what, get it done, and get it done now." I spent a lot of late nights and weekends living up to this unspoken rule. It wasn't pleasant, but, like any experience, you learn. I learned to be tough, professional, disciplined, inquisitive, and to learn things on my own without direction or guidance.

Professionally, my resume truly benefitted from the experience. I knew my packaged goods was "golden" to many personnel managers. If I wanted to get another position at another agency I could be relatively confident that I had what it took.

I wouldn't exactly say that this demand for perfection is a function only of advertising or, for that matter, a general characteristic of Grey Advertising. Many of my friends in various fields (such as investment banking) all experienced a difficult first year out of college. I'm convinced that it has a lot to do with being "freshman in the school of working life " The working world takes getting used to.

I believe not enough of us are taught to be assertive as new employees. You do have something to contribute to your job, and the company is paying you to perform that job. You don't necessarily owe the company your life. Sure you should do a good job, but you shouldn't be taken advantage of. Learning to stick up for yourself is crucial. That isn't to say you should be cocky and know-it-all. There is a happy medium. It's not like school, where you have a list of requirements to fulfill a degree. Your work is more a part of your life, and it's your decision to do with it what you will.

It took me a while to realize this. I wanted a job so badly right out of college, I felt almost indebted to Grey for offering me one. This put me in somewhat of a vulnerable position, and I didn't know any better. The academic environment of college is a far cry from the working environment, so, make sure you take the time to ask yourself what you want out of your first job. This isn't to say you need to know exactly what you're going to do for the rest of your life, but try to have a firm grip on what your expectations are.

After about 18 months at Grey, I was ready to be promoted. Timing for a promotion is usually between 13 and 18 months. In my case though, there wasn't a vacant position into which I could be promoted. At that point, I had to ask myself: one, did I want to wait and, two, did I want to continue at Grey. After a great deal of deliberation, I decided to give it a try at another firm.

In March of 1986 I went to see a few "headhunters" -- the industry's phrase for executive search/placement agencies. I went on a few interviews and was offered and accepted a position as Account Executive on a computer office products account at Needham Harper Worldwide (at that time a much smaller Agency than Grey). I really enjoyed working at a smaller agency. While you still had the advantages of sophisticated resources, there was a sense of comraderie and teamwork I had never experienced before. The President of Needham knew me by first name and I had visibility that I never would have had at Grey.

As an account person, you have a keener sense for the creative without sacrificing your marketing expertise. To me, it's the perfect mix for a challenging career and a thoroughly enjoyable profession. I'll say one thing about advertising -- I don't think you can find any other job doing the varied things you can do in this job. I mean, one minute maybe you're in production, another creative, another in marketing, another in business affairs -- another people oriented. It's really stimulating and that's fun. It's never boring.

Bibliography

Books

Advertising Age Yearbook, Crain Communications, Chicago, Illinois, annual.
A compilation of news and statistics about advertising. A good source for more in-depth research and ideas for interview questions and answers.

Careers in Marketing, David Rosenthal and Michael Powell, Prentice Hall, Englewood Cliffs, New Jersey, 1984.
Descriptive information about the types of jobs within advertising, with a special emphasis on marketing.

Choosing a Career in Business, Stephen Stumpf, Simon & Schuster, New York, New York, 1984.
Descriptive information about the types of jobs within advertising. Good comparison to other types of jobs in business.

Confessions of an Advertising Man, David Ogilvy, Atheneum, New York, New York, 1963.
David Ogilvy's diary of life in advertising. An excellent depiction of corporate culture. Required reading for those interested in working for Ogilvy & Mather Advertising.

Creative Careers, Gary Blake and Robert Bly, Wiley Press, New York, 1983.
Excellent and objective descriptive chapter on advertising. Very good bibliography.

The High-Tech Career Book, Betsy Collard, William Kaufmann Inc., Los Altos, California, 1986.
Descriptive information about the types of jobs within advertising, especially within the context of a high-tech industry.

How to Advertise, Kenneth Roman and Jane Maas, St. Martins Press, New York, New York, 1976.
Suggestions from two who have been in the advertising business and know how it works. Read this for an insight on advertising strategies.

How to Get a Job in Advertising, Ken Haas, Art Direction Book Co., New York, New York, 1979.
An excellent guide to job hunting in advertising. An insider gives more than the standard advice and offers insightful tips.

How to Put Your Book Together and Get a Job in Advertising, Maxine Paetro, Executive Communications, New York, New York, 1979.

An excellent guide for those interested in pursuing a career on the creative side of advertising as a copy writer or art director. Gives basic instructions for how to assemble a portfolio of your advertising ideas.

Inside Track, Ross and Kathryn Petras, Vintage Books, New York, 1986.

Focuses on individual companies, some in advertising, including NW Ayer, Ogilvy & Mather, J. Walter Thompson, Young & Rubicam.

Ogilvy on Advertising, David Ogilvy, Vintage Books, New York, New York, 1983.

David Ogilvy, co-founder of Ogilvy & Mather Advertising, offers his opinions about good and bad advertising. Required reading for those interested in his firm. Recommended for others who are curious about how one successful veteran thinks.

Directories

1989 Internships, F&W Publications, Cincinnati, Ohio, annual.

Describes internships and summer jobs in advertising, along with other categories. Eligibility and application information for each listing.

Advertising Career Directory, Career Publishing Corporation, New York, New York, 1985.

Excellent resource. Includes articles by industry professionals on every aspect of advertising. Also, has great listings of entry-level employers, training programs, internships. Begin your research here.

Getting Work Experience, Betsy Bauer, Dell Publishing, New York, New York, 1985.

Among other listings, describes summer internship programs in advertising. Gives pertinent application information including pay scales (if any), qualifications desired, and deadlines.

Standard Directory of Advertising Agencies (The Red Book), National Register Publishing Co., Wilmette, Illinois, three issues per year.

The directory of the advertising business. Use this to create your target list. Also, for each agency, it lists key personnel, clients, and branch offices.

Periodicals

Advertising Age, Crain Communications, Chicago, Illinois, weekly.

Considered the leading industry trade magazine.

New England Advertising Week, New England Advertising Week Inc., Boston, Massachusetts, weekly. News mostly of the Boston ad community. Contains job listings.

Chapter 8

Public Relations

Public relations is a field that is undergoing a lot of change. Many of the things we were called upon to do ten years ago can now be done in house or mechanically. Public relations in the future is not going to be press releases, it's not going to be annual reports (although all of that will be going on in some capacity). The really creative people won't be into that. What they will be into is brokering the interaction of the major institutions in the society in a way that achieves the strategic goals of one or more of these institutions ... what we're talking about is a merging of public relations and consulting.
- Jim Lichtenberg, Hill & Knowlton

Of all the mass media, public relations is the least understood. People often think of oddball stunts, scandal, and cheap tricks when they think of public relations. Also, many have a very difficult time explaining how public relations and advertising differ.

So ... what is public relations?

Industry Profile

Public relations is often best defined by the organization in which it takes place. For example, at Harvard University, public relations takes place in many offices: the alumni office, the development office, the news office, the dean's office, even the career services office.

Basically, public relations involves communicating a message to a public through a variety of means, media, and activities. The alumni office organizes and hosts a reunion; that's public relations. The development office announces a new fund drive; that's public relations. The news office publishes a campus newspaper . . . more PR. The career services office hosts an open house for freshmen and that, too, is public relations.

However, if you look at what happens in another environment, public relations becomes something entirely different. A business might try to improve its public image by sponsoring a cultural event; a press agent might try to get his client's name in the news by staging a publicity stunt; the makers of Tylenol decided to remove its capsules from the market because of a tampering scare. All of these activities lie within the realm of public relations.

We have to focus somewhere, however, so let's look at the two most active fields within public relations: public relations consultancy and corporate communications.

Public Relations Firms

Public relations firms range in size from the one-person office to very large organizations with more than 600 employees. The largest firms have annual billings of over $10 million and are located in New York City, Chicago, Los Angeles, and Washington, D.C.

Firms may have as their clients: corporations, financial institutions, governments, professional and trade associations, and academic, philanthropic and cultural organizations. Obviously, as alluded to above, these organizations have different needs. The "publics" that these organizations might want to reach would vary from stockholders and employees to legislatures and foreign governments to citizens and patrons.

The PR firm is the client's representative to the media. It develops ongoing relationships with radio and television news departments, press associations, news and feature syndicates, major business and financial publications, and daily newspapers. The public relations executives use their media contacts to funnel information from their clients to the desired audience.

PR firms, sometimes called consultancies, are consultants to their clients, performing an increasingly wider variety of services. These services might include responding to a crisis, developing a fund-raising campaign, working on a product introduction, responding to legislation, confronting merger and diversification issues, or working for a reputation change.

"Issues management" is seen as a function of growing importance for public relations firms. It entails the development of corporate strategies, looking ahead to potential dangers inherent in a course of action, and prevention of a crisis. (Now the quote at the beginning of this chapter should make more sense.)

PR firms vary in structure according to their size. A small firm would typically consist of several account executives who would each handle a number of clients. The AE would take care of all the account needs ranging from writing financial reports and speeches to arranging press conferences and publicity events. The small agency would also have a supporting staff of assistants and secretaries.

A large firm often consists of generalists organized into account teams which work on specific programs or with specific clients. These teams are often supported by a variety of specialists. Some of the special groups in a large firm might include financial relations, public affairs, marketing support, product publicity, fine arts, government relations, international relations, design/ production, research/ forecasting, creative services, public speaking, and internal communications.

Corporate Communications

Large corporations, such as IBM, AT&T, and Mobil Oil, have huge, very structured public relations divisions. These divisions exist under various names: corporate communications, corporate affairs, public affairs, public information, etc. The breadth of activity in a large company's communications division is enormous. What follow are descriptions of seven possible divisions within a large corporate communications department.

Investor/Financial Relations

This division publishes the company's prospectuses, annual and quarterly reports, and sends newsletters and financial information to stockholders. It maintains ongoing contact with the financial community, including security analysts, fund managers, and investment officers of banks.

Government Relations

Usually headquartered in Washington, D.C., this division is responsible for keeping management alerted to the latest legislative news. Company public relations specialists are often attorneys who are registered lobbyists. Some government relations divisions also coordinate political action committees.

Cultural Programs

Some large companies -- Mobil Oil for example -- are very active in this area. Mobil spends millions of dollars sponsoring and advertising selected commercial and public television programs. They also sponsor art exhibits and publish cultural magazines and books for distribution abroad. The top people in this division often have an arts or advertising background.

Press Relations

This division is the company liaison with newspapers and television. It publishes news releases, develops photographic features for newspapers or trade journals, and produces film features for television news. It usually has a staff person answering all calls from the media. Some large companies actually monitor the media to catch any valuable news breaks or "bad press." Speech writing is another function of this division.

Community Relations

Developing and maintaining a good relationship with the surrounding community and environment is the responsibility of this division. Sponsorship of educational or community projects is the usual manner of involvement. However, as is the case with large manufacturers, PR professionals in community relations may also deal with issues of environmental safety.

Employee Relations

This division is responsible for employee morale. Usually in conjunction with the personnel department, employee relations publishes company newsletters, hosts company picnics and outings, and acts as an information source for employees. The people in this division strive to get the understanding and support of employees for the company's policies.

Research and Production

The research staff checks facts and also gets involved in original research projects. The production department may produce company ads to be used in magazine campaigns. They may also produce internal and external publications.

Career Profiles

Given that there are many similarities between the functions of a corporate communications department and a PR firm, there are notable differences in the actual working situations of employees at each. An account executive at a PR firm typically works on a variety of projects for different clients, while the corporation professional usually works only within a particular area, such as financial relations.

Writing ability is one of the most essential skills a beginning PR professional must have. A clear, journalistic style is especially important because a great deal of writing is done with the press in mind. Press releases, pitch letters, annual reports, etc. are all intended for public perusal.

Of course, public speaking skills, problem solving ability, high energy, and a good sense of humor are all qualities entry-level PR pros should possess. Many firms give applicants a writing test to judge their ability to write well under a deadline. The entry-level environment requires much the same skills as those required of beginning journalists.

Account executives (AE's) working for an independent firm must work well under deadline pressure and also be able to go from one account to another smoothly and effectively. Travel and weekend work are also part of the firm's fast pace. Employment is usually less stable at an independent firm. If a small agency loses a big account, for example, people will have to be let go. There is some crossover between PR firms and corporate communications, as employees go to new jobs.

Recruiting strategies at major PR firms vary. Some only hire people with either one or two years of experience at another firm or a degree in public relations, while other large firms prefer to train college grads in their own methods.

The firms that train their own people normally hire for the account groups. Occasionally, one of the specialized groups will take on a trainee. For example, a college graduate with a concentration in international relations or government might be hired into the government relations group. When a position for a junior account executive opens up with an account group, a trainee is placed there and immediately begins work for a particular client. The trainee is under direct supervision, and learns the ropes on the job.

Typically, however, a firm will take on a college grad as an executive assistant or intern. The executive assistant is usually assigned to one account executive, with the job of helping that executive in any way possible. Depending upon the new person's talents and initiative and the health of the firm, promotion may occur within 8 to 18 months. The intern often begins work while still a student, volunteering his or her time. Upon graduation, if an opening occurs, the intern has a very good chance getting the job.

Salary

Entry-level account executives at large PR firms in New York may expect slightly more than $20,000 as a starting salary. The smaller the firm, the smaller the salary, in most cases. Earning potential, however, is great. So, in as little as three or four years, you could be earning $40,000.

Job-Hunting Tips

As with advertising, job hunting in public relations is a challenge because you are promoting yourself to experts in promotion. Therefore, begin your job hunt with as much preparation as possible.

Read all of the descriptive material you can get your hands on because it is essential that you have a good understanding of what public relations is. *The Public Relations Career Directory*, published by Career Publishing Corp., offers an excellent outline of the industry. *Opportunities in Public Relations* by Shepard Henkin is another book which gives a good basic description of the field.

Join any local professional groups, such as the Publicity Club of Boston. Student memberships are usually inexpensive, if not free. Organizations such as these often offer evening courses, seminars, workshops, scholarships, etc. for those in the field or interested in entering. Also, they are a good source of internship information.

The Public Relations Journal is the industry magazine. Read this faithfully. Also, keep in touch with general business trends by reading the *Wall Street Journal* and *Advertising Age* magazine.

Getting Experience

Internships are probably the best way to gain first-hand experience in the public relations industry. Volunteer 15-20 hours a week for a semester or during the summer. If you can spend one internship with an independent PR firm and one with a corporation, you should be able to get a good idea of the environment for which you are best suited.

A list of available internships can be found in several directories, including *The Student Guide to Mass Media Internships, 1989 Internships, Getting Work Experience,* and *The Public Relations Career Directory.*

Beyond the direct experience of an internship, working for one of the campus newspapers or magazines is good preparation. Having published writing samples will make you much more competitive in the job hunt. Also, working for a student organization publicizing an event or service is a good way to get PR experience. Be sure to save any published material you helped produce. Having samples of your work is essential.

Getting the First Job

Presenting yourself in a professional and polished manner will be of prime importance when searching for your first public relations job. Your cover letter, resume, and portfolio of writing samples must be well suited to public relations. Although public relations is a very diverse field, a general approach will not be viewed as favorably as one well focused on the goal of becoming a PR professional.

Your resume should highlight your experience in writing, organizing events, public speaking or speech writing, journalism, and any special area where you have special interest, such as government, science, high tech, public service, etc.

The cover letter should be a good example of your writing ability. Avoid the standard cover letter format, if possible. Make the letter read like a news story or, better yet, a press release. Make your future employer keep reading with interest and enthusiasm by writing an unusual letter. (See the Introduction.)

Having a portfolio of writing samples is important when applying for a job in public relations. You do not have to send the portfolio with your resume and cover letter. However, a reference should be made that you have a port- folio available. The portfolio should contain your best newswriting, any promotional writing you may have done, and a sample press release and pitch letter.

A press release is a short, usually one page, story announcing a new product or event. The release is most often sent to newspaper and magazine editors, television and radio news directors. Often, if well written, editors will print the press release as written.

A pitch letter is a longer document giving all the details about a new event, program, or product. It often provides the necessary background for a reporter to write a preliminary story, or it can prompt a reporter to do an interview.

If you don't have any published materials of your own, the best option is to create sample news releases and pitch letters. In your cover letter indicate that you would be happy to take any kind of writing test the employer might administer. Creating writing samples may seem like a great deal of work, but they will go a long way in proving your commitment to public relations.

With resume, cover letter, and portfolio in hand, you should begin contacting your career advisers. Call upon alumni advisers, family friends, and those for whom you have worked in internships to review your written materials. Also, before you visit your contacts, prepare a list of target firms. Use *O'Dwyer's Directory of Public Relations Firms* and *O'Dwyer's Directory of Corporate Communications* as your primary sources. Be sure to note the appropriate contact person, the activities and clients of the firm or department, and the size of the operation. Your career advisers may be able to provide contact names within the organizations on your list.

Begin with a mailing of 10 to 15 letters. This will give

you the opportunity to follow up your letters with phone calls and, you hope, with interviews. Cluster your mailings so that all your interviews are in one city. If you are able to arrange 7 or 8 interviews out of your first mailing, you will be doing well.

*Case Study

Cindy Berman Rowe, Public Affairs Officer

Cindy was very active in campus media groups and had spent her summers working in government and public relations firms. Her concentration was in English and government. She is now working in the communications division of the Massachusetts Budget Office.

Searching for a public relations job during senior year can be a hectic and frustrating, but ultimately rewarding experience. The following is one senior's story, documenting the various steps to follow in order to find the "perfect" opportunity.

Early Fall -- Taking the advice of my career counselor, I purchased a pocket calendar in which to note deadlines, interview times, and interviewers' names.

The next step was to get my resume in order. I assembled all the information which could be included on my resume and discussed it with the appropriate counselor. After receiving some advice on which elements to keep and how to organize them, I had my resume typeset to give it a professional look. A sharp-looking resume is a signal to your potential employer that you know how to "sell" yourself and could probably "sell" public relations or advertising ideas to other companies.

During the fall, I also started a job book - a notebook in which I listed all potential contacts and companies. The list included people for whom I had previously worked or had met through extracurricular activities.

Career Forum -- Harvard's annual career fair allows students to familiarize themselves with many companies in various fields. The Forum provides a wonderful resource for seniors who want to learn more about a particular job sector, or to explore many options. For the person interested in public relations, every company becomes a potential target because each has some kind of public relations department.

The job book I had started previously helped me in the attempt to organize all the literature and business contacts I gathered as a result of the event. It is advisable to bring several copies of your resume, both for giving to recruiters and asking their advice on how to better "advertise" yourself. Asking many questions and listening carefully to the answers can be the best introduction to the mindset of the people in a particular company. This is important information when you think about a company's PR strategy. Treat the Career Forum as a first interview: be dressed properly and be prepared to answer questions about yourself and your background.

Information Meetings -- Many companies hold information meetings before conducting interviews. Often the company representative will expect that you have attended their meetings and know something about the company and the position being offered. Another place to find this information is on the company fact sheet, a must-read before walking into an interview. The company has made an effort to provide you with information. Not taking advantage of this indicates a lack of concern. If you are interested, do your homework.

Getting Experience -- Although firms realize that they are interviewing students, candidates with previous experience have a definite advantage. Internships, during the summer or part-time during the year, often prove the best way to gaining experience in your career field. I worked in the direct mail industry during high school and during college I concentrated on expanding my public relations background. One summer I wrote, edited, and pasted-up a monthly newsletter. I worked as a press aide in a political press office the following summer, and as a community and public relations assistant the next year. These various positions taught me a great deal about the daily demands of public relations.

Extracurricular activities provide another way of gaining public relations or advertising experience. Organizing and publicizing events for a campus group will demonstrate your skill at communicating with many people. I formed a group which brought speakers from various media careers to campus. The organization also had a newsletter and working on it helped to build my writing and production skills. Writing for a college newspaper is another way to work on writing and researching skills, while at the same time proving that you can meet a deadline. This is an important message to convey to a potential employer because so much of public relations and advertising work is completed under time pressure.

Future employers will want to see samples of your writing and publicity skills. If you have worked at an internship or held a publicity-oriented extracurricular position, remember to keep samples of your writing. These will show an interviewer that you are aware of the proper form for publicity materials and that you can communicate your ideas effectively.

Job Hunting Off Campus -- Although the career

services office is a great resource, it would be a mistake to rely solely upon its recruiting system to get a job. Information interviewing - meeting with people in public relations to discuss general aspects of their jobs - can often be rewarding, and may eventually lead to a job. Although this can be a frustrating process because there is usually no position for which you are being interviewed, your contact may pass your resume on to acquaintances who do have positions available.

Answering advertisements from the newspaper, the typical job-hunting strategy, may not be effective until relatively late in the school year. Advertisers often want to hire someone "yesterday," and are unwilling to wait until June. The most effective way to land a job for a senior is through contacts. Meeting as many people as you can in public relations is the best approach.

Accepting the Job -- The main consideration in accepting a job should be what the job can offer you. Think about what the position will teach you and what this experience can lead to in the future. Talk to the company members extensively, and be clear concerning your responsibilities. Offer to spend a day in the office to get a feel for the working environment. Nothing is a sure bet, but take the time to make certain that this will be a valuable opportunity for you.

After pursuing all the above methods, I ultimately accepted a position which involved political writing. Only by going through the entire process, however, was I able to find the best opportunity.

Bibliography

Books

Careers in Marketing, David Rosenthal and Michael Powell, Prentice Hall, Englewood Cliffs, New Jersey, 1984. Does a good job at describing the different jobs within public relations, especially as they relate to marketing.

Choosing a Career in Business, Stephen Stumpf, Simon & Schuster, New York, New York, 1984.
General description of positions within public relations. Good general guide to many careers within business.

Dream Jobs, Gary Blake and Robert Bly, Wiley Press, New York, 1985.
Excellent descriptive chapter on public relations. Very good bibliography.

Inside Track, Ross and Kathryn Petras, Vintage Books, New York, 1986.
Focuses on individual companies, some in public relations, including Burson Marsteller, Carl Byoir, and Hill & Knowlton.

Directories

1989 Internships, F&W Publications, Cincinnati, Ohio, annual.
Describes internships and summer jobs in public relations, along with other categories. Eligibility and application information for each listing.

The Harvard Guide to Careers in Mass Media

Getting Work Experience, Betsy Bauer, Dell Publishing, New York, New York, 1985.

Among other listings, describes summer internship programs in public relations and advertising. Gives pertinent application information including pay scales (if any), qualifications desired, and deadlines.

O'Dwyer's Directory of Corporate Communications, J.R. O'Dwyer Co., Inc., New York, New York, annual.

The most comprehensive listing of in-house communications departments of large U.S. corporations. Lists the company executive in charge of communications, size of department, and in some cases, department budget.

O'Dwyer's Directory of Public Relations Firms, J.R. O'Dwyer Co., Inc., New York, New York, annual.

The most comprehensive listing of private public relations firms. Lists by firm, specialty, and location. Also, has information about clients, key personnel and size of firm.

Public Relations Career Directory, Career Publishing Corporation, New York, New York, 1985.

Excellent resource. Includes articles by industry professionals on every aspect of public relations. Also, has great listings of entry-level employers, training programs, internships. Begin your research here.

Index

The Job Bank series gives you . . . AMERICA'S JOBS

"Help on the job hunt . . . Anyone who is job-hunting in New York can find a lot of useful ideas in a new paperback called The New York Job Bank. . ."
— THE NEW YORK TIMES

"A timely book for Chicago job hunters follows books from the same publisher that were well received in New York and Boston . . . A fine tool for job hunters . . . For non-job hunters, the book is a pretty fair guide to Chicago's business community."
— THE CHICAGO TRIBUNE

"Job-hunting is never fun, but this book can ease the ordeal . . . The Los Angeles Job Bank will help allay fears, build confidence and avoid wheel-spinning."
— THE LOS ANGELES TIMES

17 Local Job Bank books now available

Each local Job Bank book covers a key U.S. job market with comprehensive and up-to-date information for every type of job hunter. Every Job Bank is a complete research tool for the local area, providing the necessary guidance for every step of the job search, from career choice to the initial contact to the final follow-up letter. Hundreds of listings are contained in each book. Each listing is packed with useful information:

- *Full name, mailing address, and telephone number*
- *A company personnel contact name*
- *Listings of common positions, educational background requirements, and fringe benefits offered.*
- *An industry cross-index to pinpoint employers in a particular field*
- *New Sections: Employment Forecast, Professional Associations, and Employment Services*

Qty	Description	Price	Amount
	Atlanta Job Bank, 2nd ed. 0-937860-66-2	10.95	
	Boston Job Bank, 6th ed. 1-55850-976-3	12.95	
	Chicago Job Bank, 5th ed. 1-55850-966-6	12.95	
	Dallas Job Bank, 0-937860-98-0	12.95	
	Denver Job Bank, 2nd ed. 1-55850-978-x	12.95	
	Detroit Job Bank, 0-937860-97-2	12.95	
	Florida Job Bank, 2nd ed. 1-55850-965-8	12.95	
	Houston Job Bank, 0-937860-24-7	12.95	
	Los Angeles Job Bank, 4th ed. 0-937860-89-1	10.95	
	Minneapolis Job Bank, 2nd ed. 1-55850-977-1	12.95	
	New York Job Bank, 5th ed. 1-55850-964-X	12.95	
	Ohio Job Bank, 2nd ed. 0-937860-77-8	10.95	
	Philadelphia Job Bank, 0-937860-87-5	10.95	
	San Francisco Job Bank, 4th ed. 1-55850-958-5	12.95	
	Seattle Job Bank, 1-55850-989-5	12.95	
	St. Louis Job Bank, 0-937860-99-9	12.95	
	Washington DC Job Bank, 3rd ed. 0-937860-67-0	10.95	
	1989 National Job Bank, (All 50 States) 1-55850-973-9	179.95	
	Job Bank Guide to Employment Services 1989, 1-55850-974-7	129.95	
	Shipping	2.75	2.75
		Total	

Rush me the latest editions of these books from The Job Bank Series!

Name:

Address:

City / State and Zip:

Please add $2.75 for shipping and handling to your order. Use your credit card to order by telephone, or send check or money order to:

BOB ADAMS, INC.
P U B L I S H E R S

260 Center Street, Holbrook, MA 02343 – (617) 767-8100